JOHN STEINBECK

AVAILABLE UP CLOSE TITLES:

RACHEL CARSON by Ellen Levine

JOHNNY CASH by Anne E. Neimark

ELLA FITZGERALD by Tanya Lee Stone

ROBERT F. KENNEDY by Marc Aronson

ELVIS PRESLEY by Wilborn Hampton

JOHN STEINBECK by Milton Meltzer

OPRAH WINFREY by Ilene Cooper

FRANK LLOYD WRIGHT by Jan Adkins

FUTURE UP CLOSE TITLES:

W. E. B. DU BOIS by Tonya Bolden

BILL GATES by Marc Aronson

JANE GOODALL by Sudipta Bardhan-Quallen

HARPER LEE by Kerry Madden

THURGOOD MARSHALL by Chris Crowe

UP*close*:

JOHN
STEINBECK

a twentieth-century life by
MILTON MELTZER

VIKING

VIKING
Published by Penguin Group
Penguin Young Readers Group, 345 Hudson Street, New York, New York 10014, U.S.A.
Penguin Group (Canada), 90 Eglinton Avenue East, Suite 700, Toronto, Ontario,
Canada M4P 2Y3 (a division of Pearson Penguin Canada Inc.)
Penguin Books Ltd, 80 Strand, London WC2R 0RL, England
Penguin Ireland, 25 St Stephen's Green, Dublin 2, Ireland (a division of Penguin Books Ltd)
Penguin Group (Australia), 250 Camberwell Road, Camberwell, Victoria 3124, Australia
(a division of Pearson Australia Group Pty Ltd)
Penguin Books India Pvt Ltd, 11 Community Centre, Panchsheel Park, New Delhi – 110 017, India
Penguin Group (NZ), 67 Apollo Drive, Rosedale, North Shore 0632, New Zealand
(a division of Pearson New Zealand Ltd)
Penguin Books (South Africa) (Pty) Ltd, 24 Sturdee Avenue, Rosebank, Johannesburg 2196,
South Africa

Penguin Books Ltd, Registered Offices: 80 Strand, London WC2R 0RL, England

First published in 2008 by Viking, a division of Penguin Young Readers Group

10 9 8 7 6 5 4 3 2 1

Photo credits:
Pages 18, 24, 40, 60, 139, 150, 196, 209: courtesy of the Martha Heasley Cox Center for
Steinbeck Studies, San Jose State University.
Page 70: © Time & Life Pictures/Getty Images.
Page 91: © Time & Life Pictures/Getty Images.
Page 165: Used with permission from the Stars and Stripes. © 1963, 2007 Stars and Stripes.

LIBRARY OF CONGRESS CATALOGING-IN-PUBLICATION DATA IS AVAILABLE
ISBN: 978-0-670-06139-6

Printed in the U.S.A.
Set in Goudy
Book design by Jim Hoover

CONTENTS

Foreword 11

Introduction 13

Chapter One 15

Chapter Two 41

Chapter Three 57

Chapter Four 71

Chapter Five 89

Chapter Six 109

Chapter Seven 127

Chapter Eight 146

Chapter Nine 164

Chapter Ten 184

Chapter Eleven 207

Notes 215

Books by John Steinbeck 224

Bibliography 227

Index 231

JOHN STEINBECK

FOREWORD

NO MATTER WHERE travelers go round the world, they run into people who have read John Steinbeck. His deep understanding of human emotion, his sympathy with those who have been abused or neglected, his defense of their struggle for a decent standard of living, have made him one of our most beloved authors. So powerful was his writing that it earned him the world's highest award for literature, the Nobel Prize.

Yet no one could have predicted this would be in young Steinbeck's future. For he was the classic school dropout, and for a long time had great trouble earning a living as a writer. Strangely, fifteen years after the publication of *The Grapes of Wrath*, his enormously popular novel about migrant farm workers, he wrote, "Writers are a sorry lot. The best you can say of them is

that they are better than actors and that's not much."
And "Wish to God I could learn to write as I would
like to write. I fall so damn short every time. But I'll
keep plugging and damn it—one day I'll maybe turn
up something."

That he did turn up something—and far more than
once—makes us want to know how it happened.

How did a man who struggled so hard to get the
right words down on paper do it?

INTRODUCTION

I READ *The Grapes of Wrath* the year it was published. It was the summer of 1939. I had just lost my job, and with two other jobless friends, we drove across the land in a beat-up old car, reading aloud to one another from the pages of that beautiful and shocking story. Into the great Dust Bowl region we wandered, seeing the remnants of farms abandoned by desperate families, and then on to California, where we stopped at the camps of migrant farm workers struggling like the Joad family in Steinbeck's novel to survive.

Me, too, I thought then, maybe someday I'll be able to write what will move people to make this land of ours a better home for all. I never thought then that someday, many years later, I'd have the chance to write the story of John Steinbeck himself. I've written biographies of such earlier authors as Hawthorne, Melville, and Whitman. Now I want to try my hand at one of the great writers of my own time.

ONE

SALINAS?

Who ever heard of that place?

Maybe not you, but millions of people around the world who've read the stories of John Steinbeck. He often mentions his hometown in California. Nothing important about it, except that it's where he was born on February 27, 1902.

What was the United States like at that time? The population was 76 million, almost one-fourth of what it would be in 2000. After winning the Spanish-American War, America had taken over Spain's colonies in the Caribbean and the Philippines. Helped by the expanding markets overseas, the economy boomed.

New technology spurred industrial growth. Expert craftsmen, no longer needed, were replaced by the unskilled. Business mergers placed control of industry in fewer hands. Millions of new jobs—unskilled and lower-paying—were filled by women, children, new immigrants and migrants.

Labor struggles that had dominated the news since the 1870s continued into the early twentieth century. Not only working people but the middle class, too, sensed that reforms were needed. Crusading newspapers and muckraking magazines did much to expose the abuses of power by corporations as well as political bosses.

Theodore Roosevelt, becoming president in 1901, fought the corruption of politics by business, upheld the antitrust laws, defended the rights of labor, and campaigned for conservation of our natural resources.

There were only 2,500 people living in Salinas when John was born. The town sits in the great coastal valley of California, a landscape remarkable only for its flatness.

You'd think nothing special would come out of so ordinary a place. But Steinbeck, the veteran author, saw in it "the whole nasty bloody lovely history of the world."

It's the ordinary that most of us tend to dismiss. What's special about ordinary people? we ask. Everything, he'd answer. Their humanness, the way they talk, think, move, swear, laugh, get mad, work, get drunk, fight, make love, raise kids, grow old, die. You recognize his keen eye, his sensitive ear, his understanding heart perhaps best of all in his classic novel *The Grapes of Wrath.*

Steinbeck was the third child and only son of John Ernst Steinbeck and Olive Hamilton Steinbeck. Before him came his sisters Esther and Beth, and after him, Mary. John's paternal grandfather, a cabinetmaker in Germany, had come to the United States, eventually settling in California after the Civil War. His maternal grandfather, Samuel Hamilton, emigrated from Ireland as a teenager, married an American girl of Irish ancestry, and moved on to California, where he made his living as a skilled blacksmith.

John's mother taught school in her youth. One-room schools these were, crammed with kids of all ages trying to learn a dozen different subjects. His father was an accountant who managed a flour mill in Salinas. When the company shut it down, he opened

Here we are. Mary, John & Jill — Salinas Aug 28.07

Steinbeck, age five, with his sister Mary, age two, on the red pony
named Jill, 1908.

a store selling feed and grain. But with transportation
by horse and buggy giving way to the new automobiles
and tractors, the enterprise failed. These two disap-
pointments in a row made Mr. Steinbeck fearful of the
future. Things picked up when a friend who managed
a sugar factory close by Salinas got him the job as its
bookkeeper. Not long after, the treasurer of Monterey
County died. Influential friends had Mr. Steinbeck
appointed to fill out the term. It was a respectable,
decent-paying job, and he did so well he was reelected
to that office again and again.

John's father loved gardening, raised chickens, and

kept a horse. When John turned four, his father gave him a Shetland pony called Jill, ordering the child to learn to take care of it himself. In that family you were expected to know what to do, how to do it, and when to do it. Though no feminist, his mother did not think that only girls should be trained for the domestic chores. John, like his sisters, had to do the dusting, mopping, cleaning, and laundry. Yet at times he could be so stubbornly resistant, so lazy, it enraged his mother. You can imagine her shrugging: what could such a kid grow up to be? A nothing?

When he was middle-aged and a parent himself, Steinbeck recalled his father's and mother's influence on him. His father, he said, was a restless and "singularly silent man, strong, rather than profound. Cleverness only confused him." Yet in the son's struggle to be a writer, "it was he who supported and backed me and explained me—not my mother. She wanted me desperately to be something decent, like a banker. . . . But my father wanted me to be myself. . . . I think he liked the complete ruthlessness of my design to be a writer in spite of mother and hell."

Salinas grew on top of swampland, and as the

swamps were drained, richly productive soil brought the town prosperity. Cattle ranching was the first enterprise to prosper. Then came the planting of sugar beets and the rise of a sugar factory. But it was lettuce that became the "green gold" of the Valley. The town's population soon doubled and then redoubled, with wooden-frame houses springing up on each side of what is now South Main Street. The upper-crust families lived on one side and the lower on the other side.

California, in John's childhood, was one of the newer states of the Union—only some fifty years old. The United States had acquired a vast territory, some of which became California, through its war against Mexico. By the peace treaty of 1846 that ended the war, Mexico ceded not only a huge territory but also the 75,000 Mexican people living on it to the United States.

For a child, the California landscape was an unending delight: the redwoods, the mountains and valleys, the infinite stretch of shoreline, with the bays, estuaries, and beaches. And the wildlife! Deer, mountain lion, wildfowl, sea animals in uncountable number.

Salinas was so small that when you strolled the streets you knew just about everyone you passed. Many were poor, some were rich. As he grew older, John thought those who acquired wealth weren't any happier than before. They had nothing more to do than chase after more money. And one way to get rich was to acquire big tracts of land and plant crops the world needed to live on.

Lettuce, that was it! The cold and foggy weather provided several crops a year of what Salinas folk bragged was the best lettuce anywhere. The development of mechanical refrigeration soon made it possible for refrigerated freight cars to move the lettuce (and other crops, too) toward the highly profitable marketing centers of such cities as Chicago and New York.

John spent summers at the beach. He learned to swim very early. He liked to walk along the shore, gathering specimens of marine life. Weekends in the spring and fall and on summer vacations the family went to a small cottage Mr. Steinbeck had bought near Monterey, at Pacific Grove. Sardine canneries were crowded along the shore. Throughout his life, John would view the cottage as a seasonal home. So close by the sea he would feel "an electric excitement." Occasionally during summer vacations he would visit with the Hamilton wing of the family on their ranch about sixty miles south of Salinas. In several of his books you can see what he learned about horses and cattle and the routine of farmwork.

Mrs. Steinbeck, unlike her husband, was a community leader, active in charities, always concerned to relieve poverty and correct injustice. Neighbors said she had high hopes for her son. But she worried about his tendency to be a loner, and pushed him to join things he shied away from. John was closer to the women of the family than to his father, a withdrawn man given to long stretches of silence. Yet the son would write of his father: "My father was a great man, as any lucky man's father must be. . . . He taught me—glory to God, honor to my family, loyalty to my friends, respect for the law, love of country and instant and open revolt against tyranny, whether it comes from the bully in the schoolyard, the foreign dictator, or the local demagogue."

His mother encouraged the free play of his imagination. She told him bedtime stories of magical works or read him poetical narratives. She saw to it that there were lots of books around the house—like *Treasure Island*, *Ivanhoe*, *The Last of the Mohicans*. Passages from the Bible and Shakespeare's plays became familiar. Best of all for John were the thrilling adventures of King Arthur and the knights of the Round Table. He found them in a book an aunt gave him by Sir Thomas Malory, an Englishman of the fifteenth century. It was as though a door had been opened to a rich secret language. With his younger sister Mary, he would play at acting out the medieval tales.

Music meant much to the Steinbecks. Classical recordings were often played. John developed so strong a love for music that much later when he began to write, he'd have music going to help set the tone, the mood, the rhythm he needed.

In the early 1900s, very few children went on to high school, and an even tinier percentage entered college. But John's mother paid no attention to limits others set. She insisted her children work hard to get good grades, paving the way for college.

Long after finishing grammar school, John recalled just one character from those days. His best friend in

An elementary school class photograph with Steinbeck in the last row, sixth from the right, circa 1908.

the fourth grade was Pickles Moffet, he said. "He was an almost perfect little boy for he could throw rocks harder and more accurately than anyone, he was brave beyond belief in stealing apples or raiding the cake section in the basement of the Episcopal church. Pickles had only one worm in him. The writing of a simple English sentence would put him in a state of shock very like that condition which we now call battle fatigue."

Finishing grammar school, John went on to Salinas

High School. He was a big kid by now, not tall, but bulky. Wide shoulders, deep chest, still some signs of baby fat, and jug ears. "When I was 16 or 17," he recalled, "I spent a lot of goodly time looking in the mirror bemoaning my ugliness, turning my head to see whether some position or other wouldn't soften the coarseness of my features. None of them did." There was little to remember him by in those high school years. He wasn't one of those eager beavers always volleying out the answers. He managed to get decent, if not outstanding grades. One teacher, however, thought his English compositions were so good she read them aloud to the students. Maybe it was Miss Cupp who planted the seed that grew into a profession.

The students were asked to read widely in great literature: George Eliot, Thomas Hardy, Dostoyevsky, Flaubert. Later John said that "I remember them not at all as books but as things that happened to me."

The curriculum also took in history, economics, math, science, Latin, and Spanish, all of it in preparation for possible entry into college. It was a small high school—only twenty-five students in the senior class—so it was easy to find a place in school activities.

John went in for track and basketball as well as the dramatic club, but was no shining light in any of these. He did best writing witty articles for the yearbook.

His social life in those years? It was pretty much a zero. He made some friends among the boys and none among the girls. They just ignored him.

His junior year brought a personal crisis. He was one of the millions hit by a flu epidemic. In his case it turned into a siege of pneumonia and came close to killing him. He felt so horrible he was ready to give up. But his mother wouldn't tolerate a quitter. She ordered him to get out of bed. And he did.

The last years of high school were marked by the terrible catastrophe of World War One. The United States was drawn into it in 1917, when John was fifteen. No one knew how long the war might last, and how many more soldiers would be needed, so high-school boys were given uniforms and rifles, drilled in formations, and taken out to a firing range for target practice. The drafting of men to fight produced a shortage of labor for agriculture. The students were also on call when planting or harvesting time came round. John picked fruit or hoed beans for long stretches, paid thirty-five cents an hour for his labor. The war would end before he was old enough to join up.

Many years later, thinking it would be good for his teenage son Thom to get a summer job, Steinbeck recalled wanting to do a man's work himself at that age. He wrote a friend on a Texas ranch, asking if he could employ Thom, and then said:

> When I was sixteen I differed with my parents and walked away and got a job on a ranch where they didn't give a damn whether I was sixteen or not. I slept in the bunk house with all the other hands, got up at four-thirty, cleaned my stall, and saddled or harnessed my horses depending on the job, ate my beefsteak for breakfast and went to work, and the work day was over when you could no longer see. I learned a great deal on that job, things I have been using ever since. I got a sense of values I have never lost but above all I became free. Once I could do that, make my own pay with my own hands, nobody could ever push me around again. Also I learned about men,

how some are good and some are bad, and how most are some of both.

And I learned about money, and how hard it is to get. On that ranch there wasn't one soul who knew me or my family or gave a damn. It wouldn't have been as good if there had been. I think that until a boy is put out on his own, he hasn't a chance to be a man. A kind of pride comes with it that is never lost again and a kind of humility also. I think the best gift I could give my son is that fierce sense of independence. Very few American kids ever get the chance to have it. They are always able to come up with excuses. But there aren't any excuses on a man's job. You do it or you don't.

John began to write probably in his first year of high school. It was not what his teachers required of him, only what he himself wanted to try his hand at. Earlier he had written verses as his way of commenting on happenings or birthdays. The writing turned more serious as he entered high school. He would sit alone in his upstairs bedroom and sweat out a short story. Then he'd corner a friend or a neighbor, and whether they were interested or not, insist on reading his piece aloud.

That practice—reading his work to others—would continue throughout his life. He did it not only to find out what others thought, but to distance himself—as though sitting in judgment on someone else's work.

The love of language seemed born in him. The sound of words, the history of words, the images they conjured up, helped to mold the kind of writer he grew up to be. Success—whether in his own eyes or through acceptance for publication—would not come easily. He learned to develop the inner armor that protected him from disapproval and rejection.

Oddly, he would often misspell words and misuse punctuation. Even when he became famously successful, the errors continued.

With that strong drive to write, it might seem natural to enter college as an English major. Not to John. He wasn't eager to go. What could the sheltered life of a student do to broaden his experience? He'd rather ship out on a freighter. His parents didn't see it that way. They knew their son wanted to be a writer, but weren't at all sure he'd make it. They'd managed to send his older sisters to college, and he must go, too.

The choice was the nearby campus of Stanford University, in Palo Alto. Do well there and then he'd be fit to enter some respectable profession or business.

So at seventeen he did try college life, yet in his own peculiar on-and-off way. He would take courses now and then for the next six years—and then quit without a degree. The record shows he missed classes, dropped out, returned, made the grades, failed—and then the same all over again.

This erratic path in the academic world wasn't unique for writers. Others, including the best—such as the poet Robert Frost or the novelist F. Scott Fitzgerald—stumbled over a similar rocky path. They couldn't accept the demands of academic life.

It doesn't mean the college years were wasted. An artist's success isn't measured by academic standards. John did learn much at Stanford. To follow him during those years is like twisting through a maze. Solid facts are that he made good friends—and long-lasting ones, too—and benefited from his connection with some fine teachers in his preferred field of literature.

Yet only a few months after classes began, his

parents were notified that John was not living up to his potential. What he was doing a lot of was playing poker in the dorm, staying up all night in bull sessions, and turning to alcohol to lift himself out of bouts of depression. Weekends when he refused to return home to Salinas, he'd party with pals in nearby San Francisco.

He probably did less of this than he bragged about to make himself appear to be a romantic character like the writer Jack London, whom he so admired. When his first summer vacation came, Mr. Steinbeck got John and his roommate George Mors temporary jobs lugging heavy equipment for a surveying expedition in the mountains. A few weeks of that and they quit. Then Papa, still loyal, had them taken on as maintenance men for the Spreckels sugar plant in Salinas.

Spreckels was by now a big outfit, having expanded beyond its basic job of raising beets for sugar production. It owned or leased ranches where beef cattle were raised. Besides the full-time staff, there were seasonal hires of migratory ranch hands. "Bindlestiffs," they were called. They roamed California seeking work, ready to do anything at all in return for small pay.

Getting to know such men fed John's imagination. He quarried them for characters, incidents, talk, conflicts, love affairs, crimes. Much of what he learned found expression years later in his short stories and novels. This was a more exciting education than a Stanford classroom provided. Most of the bindlestiffs he met in these early years were of Anglo-Saxon origin. But a swelling tide of migrants was rolling in from Mexico and the Philippines in search of work. You meet Mexicans like this especially in *Tortilla Flat*, a novel he would write later.

Working on ranches, John met labor organizers who argued that socialism was the answer to the poverty the migrants suffered. Why in this land of plenty did so many people go hungry? The issue troubled him, though he never felt socialism would work "so long as such narrowness and greed as I have seen exist."

John's second year at Stanford began badly. He fell so far behind in his studies that he was put on probation. He would go to classes only now and then, preferring to spend more of his time in the university library. There he could read what he wanted, not what a professor demanded. Far from being idle, he wrote furiously, too. John completed six short stories in that first term. Sadly, they've never been found.

By midterm his record was so poor that his parents were told that John had two weeks to shape up. John couldn't, or wouldn't. He left his dorm, took a bus to San Francisco, and holed up in a flophouse. He hung around seamen's hiring halls hoping to find a berth on some merchant vessel bound for the Far East. No luck. Then he got a clerk's job in a department store that was adding staff for the Christmas rush. When that was over, so was the job.

What now? Nothing. Broke and hungry, no place to go but home. Luckily his parents wisely let him alone. Still, he couldn't stay on at his childhood home. Again, he was rescued by Spreckels. He was hired at one of their ranches to be foreman of a gang of Mexican and Filipino migrant workers. By this time—the 1920s—Mexican labor was becoming the mainstay of California's agricultural army. At least 150,000 Mexicans were following the state's crops. The *braceros*, as the Mexicans were called, handled cotton, fruit, sugar beets, and vegetables with great skill. And as America's eating habits changed, the state's growers profited by it.

The work was grindingly heavy. He pitched in to help load big sacks of sugar beets onto the trucks that carried them into Salinas. His hands blistered and his back ached terribly. Four months of this harsh routine was all he could take. He quit, went home again, and hid in his bedroom, to sit alone, reading or writing.

When his deep fatigue wore off, he found odd jobs in and around Salinas. It was mostly manual labor for little pay, but at least room and board were free. His mother still ruled the roost and had little patience for her boy's erratic behavior. When she railed at him, his father would retreat into another room to hide himself in silence behind his newspaper.

So John left home again and returned to Stanford. You couldn't say his many months away from school were wasted. He was learning how other people lived, what their dreams and illusions were, how they got along, or how they failed. It was all seeds planted in a fertile imagination. He stored away in scribbled notes the things he learned about people, and would bring them to life on the pages of the books to come.

That Stanford would allow so odd a dropout to

reenter was astonishing. He must have guaranteed he'd do it right this time. Luckily he found his way into a group of like minds who called themselves the English Club. He became a close friend of two older students, Webster Street and Carl Wilhelmson, both veterans of the world war just ended, and, like John, planning careers as writers.

A third new friend was Carlton Sheffield, who became his roommate. He, too, was aspiring to be a writer. These hopefuls, with others at times, would sit for hours in the dorm or at eating joints off campus and argue fiercely about their favorite author. Was it Sinclair Lewis? Sherwood Anderson? Jack London? Upton Sinclair? John would dominate the discussion, because he seemed to have read everything and was cocksure about what was good and what wasn't.

Two women on the staff of the English department made their mark on Steinbeck. Professor Margery Bailey was a fiercely demanding teacher you didn't dare attempt to offer fakery. She and John became good friends. Another professor, Edith Mirrielees, was gentler. She told John his work was good enough to be published, but she didn't know where.

Years later, Professor Mirrielees set down her ideas on what makes for good writing in a book called *The Story Writer*. It must have been the same advice she gave to John and his classmates:

> The "lean terse style" is one towards which most beginners can profitably struggle. . . . For most stories and most writers, deliberate ornamentation needs much scrutiny before it is allowed a place in finished work. Phrases pushing up like mushrooms above the level of the narrative have a habit of turning out to be toadstools on later inspection. "Take out whatever you particularly like" is hard counsel, but oftener than not it is wise counsel as well.

What she warned against—overwriting, sentimentality—were faults critics would accuse John of later on. But right now he was writing all the time, it seemed. And again, he would thrust himself upon any friend and read a piece aloud in his deep voice. If you dared interrupt him he'd rush out of the room. He didn't want criticism; he just wanted you to listen. But as one friend said, you wanted to listen, for his stories were really good.

By now John had become a self-disciplined writer. He worked at it every day, usually setting aside the morning hours, when he felt his energy was at its peak. Two of his stories were published in the *Stanford Spectator* in 1924. One of them, centering on a retarded teenage girl, foreshadows the sympathetic concern for handicapped people evident in his later work.

In a letter to a friend he mentioned writing short stories that spring, saying, "one was perfectly rotten, two were fair, three were quite good. About the only thing that can be said for them is that they do not resemble anything which has ever been written."

The seed of John's intense interest in marine biology was planted when he took a summer course at the university's Hopkins Marine Station. He studied a rich variety of marine creatures in their natural habitat in Monterey Bay. It required long hours in the lab, field trips, and collecting expeditions. His work in marine biology led him to see humans as a part of the whole sphere of nature—not isolated and separate, not unique, but shaped by and responsive to all life. He was one of the rare writers of his century who framed his characters within an ecological perspective.

In the summer of 1924, John was back in Salinas. He and his friend Sheffield worked at a branch plant of Spreckels till mid-August, quit, took their meager savings, and bummed around San Francisco for a while.

They returned to Stanford for the winter and spring semesters of 1925. This time John wanted no part of dormitory restrictions. He holed up instead in a shack attached to a stable. There was no stove, no water, no electricity. The rent? Five dollars a month. He slept on a cot, washed where and when he could, propped his typewriter on an orange crate, and resumed his writing. One of his sisters dropped in on him and found it disgusting. Don't tell Mother, he urged.

The work began with first drafts in longhand, set down on the lines of old ledgers from his father's office. He always used a very small script, hard for others to read. Then came revisions or second drafts, perhaps on the battered old typewriter. Several of the stories he wrote then survive. They show he was experimenting, trying to do what no other writer had done. What he was after was a unique and distinctive voice. He was less concerned with style than with the creation of unconventional characters in unusual situations.

When the spring session ended, he had not completed enough courses to qualify for a degree. He wanted no more of Stanford and dropped out, for good this time. What to do next?

TWO

JOHN DECIDED HE'D like to try life in New York City. But he'd need money to get there and make a fresh start. That summer of 1925 he found work doing odd chores at a holiday resort lodge near Lake Tahoe. It would leave him the time to continue writing and to plan for whatever might lie ahead.

With the summer over and the guests gone, John left the lodge and returned to Salinas. Saying good-bye to his parents, once again he roamed the San Francisco waterfront. Then he traveled down to Los Angeles, where he booked passage on the *Katrina*. Coasting down the California shore and through the Panama Canal, it stopped for two days in Panama City. (The tiny town would be the setting for his first published novel, *Cup of Gold*.) Aboard ship he struck

Steinbeck while he was a student at Stanford.

up a friendship with the illustrator Mahlon Blaine. Of course Blaine had to read what John had written. And luckily, he liked it enough to help John find a publisher for *Cup of Gold*, years later.

His father had given John a hundred dollars for expenses, and when the freighter stopped again, this time in Havana, John, who had taken to drinking early, blew most of it in the local bars. Then the last stop: New York. He went ashore with empty pockets, lucky to lodge with his newly married sister Beth in her tiny Brooklyn flat. Within a week he found a job with a construction company that was building the new Madison Square Garden on Eighth Avenue and Fiftieth Street. The Garden would become famous as America's chief indoor arena. Championship prize fights, hockey matches, cowboy rodeos, national political conventions, the six-day bicycle race, and the Barnum and Bailey Circus were among the annual spectacles. The job was no cinch: he pushed big wheelbarrows heavy with wet cement up a ramp to where masons laid brick on lofty scaffolding. He often worked a fifteen-hour day, and, reaching his Brooklyn room late at night, would flop into bed too tired to eat supper.

He hadn't the energy even to read the newspaper, much less to write. After about six weeks, when a fellow worker plummeted to his death from a scaffold, John quit. Such work couldn't be combined with a writing career. Family helped him out of this hole. His uncle Joe Hamilton, a Chicago advertising executive, visiting the city on business, met and liked John. He offered him a job in his Chicago agency. No, this wouldn't do. How could grinding out ad copy benefit his own writing? Nor did he want to leave New York. Okay, said his uncle, and promptly got John taken on as a reporter by friends on the staff of Hearst's newspaper, the New York *American*. Many a young writer believed work on a newspaper would benefit his career. Theodore Dreiser, Stephen Crane—they'd done it. And Ernest Hemingway, too.

John's sister nudged him out of her cramped quarters and he moved into a run-down old tenement near Gramercy Park. His friend Mahlon Blaine lived there, too, and they began going out on the town together. It was now that John fell for a showgirl he met in a Greenwich Village restaurant. The affair soon faded, for she wanted a lover on the rise in the business world, not a struggling reporter who dreamed of becoming a novelist.

At the *American,* John was sent to Brooklyn and Queens to track down stories, but he got lost too often, and was reassigned to cover the Federal Court in lower Manhattan. He hung around with the other reporters, covering trials and playing bridge in dull hours. His writing wasn't the crisp, direct style the paper wanted, but rather the fancy prose editors detested, and he was fired.

The family took the news badly. Couldn't he do anything right? Would he ever earn his own way?

Without a job, without a girlfriend. It didn't upset John. Now he could hole up in his room, and set to work on the novel that would become *Cup of Gold*—a story about Sir Henry Morgan (1635–88), the most famous buccaneer of his time. Instead of being hanged for his many crimes, Morgan was knighted by Charles II, king of England, and made deputy governor of Jamaica, a British island in the Caribbean.

Scribbling away on something he loved doing was fine, but still he had to eat and pay rent. Blaine offered help. He took several of John's short stories to a friend in a small publishing house. The editor liked the work, and told John if he'd add another batch, they'd publish the collection.

John was thrilled. A professional had stamped "quality" on his work. He put aside the pirate novel and wrote several new stories, mostly rising out of his brief life in New York. He then retyped the entire manuscript and delivered it personally to the publisher's office. He was shocked to find the editor who'd encouraged him had left the company. Shown into another editor's office, he was asked if he had a contract. No, said John, but he thought he had a commitment. The editor shook his head at this novice's innocence, and sent him away. He didn't even ask to see the stories.

Bitterly disappointed, and broke, what could he do now? No manual labor job this time. Nor did he feel he could beg his uncle to help him again. He'd had enough of the big city. Maybe he'd be better off back in California. Luckily he was able to make a deal on the waterfront. In return for working as an assistant steward serving meals on a freighter heading for San Francisco via the Panama Canal, he'd be given his passage.

By mid-June of 1926, at the age of twenty-four,

he was home in Salinas. The family welcomed him warmly, despite doubt that their son could ever earn a living as a writer. His father tried to get him to see that most writers, no matter how good, are unable to support themselves and a family on literary earnings. No, not me, John felt. He wouldn't do any work that would keep him from his goal. Not even marriage must stand in the way. When his writer-friend Carlton Sheffield had married, John thought it a bad mistake, not because he had anything against the wife but because marriage itself would block a writer's path to his goal.

John visited with old friends around Palo Alto for a few days, then went up to Lake Tahoe in search of a job. This time he was taken on as caretaker of the large estate of Mrs. Alice Brigham, a wealthy widow. He was given the caretaker's cabin, a comfortable setup for sleeping and writing. When her family left around mid-October, he had the place all to himself. He even had access to the family's large collection of English and American literature.

It was a lonely time for him, and a challenging one. He had struggled to write stories among the millions in Manhattan, all bent on going their own way. Now he had the solitude needed to find his own voice.

"Solitude" was a theme Henry David Thoreau touched on in his classic *Walden; or, Life in the Woods*. It was a book John cherished, marking favorite passages, such as this:

> I have never felt lonesome, or in the least oppressed, by a sense of solitude, but once, and that was a few weeks after I came to the woods, when, for an hour, I doubted if the near neighborhood of man was not essential to a serene and healthy life. To be alone was something unpleasant. But I was at the same time conscious of a slight insanity in my mood, and seemed to foresee my recovery. In the midst of a gentle rain while these thoughts prevailed, I was suddenly sensible of such sweet and beneficent society in Nature, in the very pattering of the drops, and in every sound and sight around my house, an infinite and unaccountable friendliness all at once like an atmosphere sustaining me, as made the fancied advantages of human neighborhood insignificant, and I have never thought of them since.

John would find time and again that he needed to get away to do his best work. Somehow he would find the right retreat in whatever part of the world he was in at the time.

There was lots of work to do to maintain the Brigham estate in good condition, everything from draining pipes to mending fences. He kept working on his novel *Cup of Gold*, but when he felt blocked, turned for relief to short stories. One of these, set in a mythic land, he sent to a small magazine under a pen name (because he doubted the story was very good) and to his astonishment it got into print in March 1927. It was his first professional publication, and paid him all of seven dollars.

That winter he made a new friend, Lloyd Shebley, a naturalist for California's Department of Fish and Game. They shared a great interest in marine life and spent much time studying the breeding habits of fish.

Meanwhile John was back at his novel, bragging to Sheffield that he was writing three to four thousand words a day. He thought he had done some very fine writing, but then decided that much of it wasn't so good. To other friends he wrote that he was bound to

create something beautiful, and that he was willing to work for many years with no success if only he could one day reach what he aspired to.

Comments he made from time to time on the work of other writers, even the most highly valued, suggest that he didn't care for fancy writing or wit. He sought for himself a well-told story with a steadfast moral point of view.

When the Brigham family returned in May, John took a leave to visit his family in Salinas. It wasn't a happy homecoming. Where was the fruit of all these years? He was twenty-five now and what had he done with his life? His mother stormed at him till he walked out in a rage.

He returned to his job at the Brigham estate. That fall and winter he used almost every hour after his chores to move ahead with the novel, seldom seeing anyone. In January 1928, he finished a draft, and sent chapters to various friends, seeking their criticism, and often accepting it.

In a letter to Sheffield, he said that after finishing *Cup of Gold*, he let it stand a while, then read it over, and found that it was no good. John would experience

this bleak mood again and again throughout his life. He rarely believed what he'd done was really good. The world knows that he was wrong.

John bundled up the manuscript of *Cup of Gold* and sent it off to an old Stanford friend, Ted Miller, now a lawyer living in New York. Miller had offered to act as John's agent in finding a publisher. Through his friend Lloyd Shebley, he found a new job as Shebley's assistant at a fish hatchery in Tahoe City. He would feed the freshly hatched trout and conduct tours of the hatchery, a tourist attraction. The two men shared a house nearby. John would be paid $345 for three months work, a handsome sum, he thought.

In mid-June Carol Henning and her sister Idell dropped in to see the hatchery. Carol—a tall, slender, vivacious woman—and John hit it off at once. That night the two sisters double-dated with John and Shebley—dinner, then dancing under the stars till midnight.

John fell in love with Carol. The sisters stayed for over a week, and John saw Carol as often as his work permitted. When she had to leave, he felt devastated. How could he live without this wonderful woman? Yet

he was in no position to marry anyone. It depressed him. He knew he was not handsome, and this may have caused him to doubt that any woman would want him for more than a casual date. He took to drinking too much, and this only made matters worse.

His emotions could be so strong that he'd lose control and make a difficult moment much worse. For instance, on one occasion during his time at the hatchery, a young woman rebuffed a pass he made at her. He seemed to go crazy, yelled at her, dragged her to the second-story window of his house, and dangled her by the ankles from the window. She screamed for help. Luckily Shebley was nearby; he raced to the window and rescued her.

The girl fled, and Shebley worked frantically to sober up his friend. He told John what an idiot he was; he could have killed the girl. The next day, the effects of alcohol worn off, Steinbeck sent Shebley to the girl's cabin to apologize deeply for what he'd done. Amazingly, she not only forgave him but agreed to go out with him that evening.

John didn't quite make it through the summer at the hatchery. He was fired for wrecking the superintendent's new pickup truck. He packed his belongings and left for San Francisco. It was late September of 1928 when he arrived. No job in sight, no money to live on. And in his mind, stray thoughts about a second novel—and the prospect of seeing Carol Henning again.

He found a room in an old tenement and then a job doing manual labor for a company manufacturing hempen bags—not much different from the heavy work at Madison Square Garden. Carol meanwhile was taken on by the business department of the *San Francisco Chronicle*. They both worked long hours, six days a week. It left little time for the pleasures the town offered.

John kept writing in the evenings, this time on a mystical novel set in California. Carol's friends on the newspaper drew her into a group interested in socialism, and John sometimes joined them to discuss the coming revolution.

But rebellious as he often was, he'd never go down that road. He was too much an individualist, too independent to submit to the political doctrine of socialism.

Young people, and older ones, too, thought America's capitalist system, where private ownership of factories, farms, mines, railroads, and other businesses prevailed, was the root cause of the rapidly growing gap between rich and poor. They believed that public ownership of the means of production would solve the nation's social and economic problems. Some people looked to the Soviet Union, which had been created by a communist revolution in Russia in 1917, and held it up as the model for a socialist America. Few at the time foresaw the terrible direction the Soviet Union would take.

Worn out by the heavy labor at the warehouse, John quit. His father stepped in to help. He offered his son the use of the family cottage at Pacific Grove, plus twenty-five dollars a month for as long as he might need it. (It was possible back then for two people to barely get by on that monthly sum.) For John the gift was not only a lifesaver; it meant his family at last believed in his future as a writer, perhaps because he was so persistent in trying to fulfill his dream.

Carol came to visit him often on weekends at Pacific Grove. Now it felt like a honeymoon cottage, though he resisted her gentle push toward marriage.

He wasn't ready for that responsibility. Then in 1929 came great news from Ted Miller. He had got the publisher Robert McBride to take *Cup of Gold*! John would receive an advance of $250. It was the first time his writing had earned him real money. That seven other publishers had turned down the novel was quickly forgotten.

Cup of Gold tells the story of young Henry Morgan, the pirate, trying to find his way in the world. When he reaches his cup of gold, he is no longer sure this is what he wants. The novel shifts in tone from the elaborate and precious to the realistic, direct prose that would later characterize his better work. It was more fantasy than historical novel. Steinbeck was trying out different voices.

Different voices? Different personalities? In a letter around this time to a college friend, A. Grove Day, he said:

> You will remember that at Stanford I went about being different characters. I even developed a theory that one had one personality in essence, that one was a reflection of a mood

plus the moods of other persons present. I wasn't pretending to be something I wasn't. For the moment I was truly the person I thought I was.

Published in August, that first novel was pretty much ignored by the press. It drew some brief reviews, and almost no praise, selling very few copies.

In the fall John moved back to San Francisco. Though he enjoyed Pacific Grove, he missed the busy life of the city. And he hoped to put aside enough money to allow a full-time return to his writing.

He moved into Carl Wilhelmson's small apartment, sharing the cramped space with this friend who'd already published a first novel and had a second signed up. They had lots to talk about, especially the work of the two newest literary stars, Ernest Hemingway and William Faulkner, both only a few years older than John. John was reading Hemingway now, whose short stories *In Our Time* (1925) and novel *The Sun Also Rises* (1926) had made a huge impact by the originality of their style.

Now John and Carol decided to get married. The

Steinbecks were pleased. They liked Carol, the way she helped John, talking over his problems with him, typing his manuscripts over and over, correcting his spelling and punctuation. She was an energetic, talented person who gave up pursuing a career of her own to help manage his. Her spirit would carry them through the early years of bad times they did not know lay ahead.

On January 14, 1930, John and Carol were married in Glendale. No parents were present, only Sheffield and his wife. They celebrated by buying a puppy, a Belgian sheepdog. For fifteen dollars a month the newlyweds rented a crumbling little stucco house in Eagle Rock, near Los Angeles. With the help of friends they labored long to patch it up into a livable home. Later John would recall that they were "as starved and happy a group as ever robbed an orange grove. I can still remember the dinners of hamburger and stolen avocados."

THREE

JUST BEFORE JOHN and Carol married, one of the great calamities of American history occurred— the sudden collapse of the country's entire economic structure when the stock market crashed in October 1929. It signaled the beginning of a decade-long period of widespread unemployment and poverty that would become known as the Great Depression.

Within two months, several million people lost their jobs. Many businesses came to a dead halt. Being jobless meant doing without necessities—physical deprivation. But being without work did terrible damage to the human spirit, too.

The deepest wounds of the depression were borne by children. Years of poverty, hunger, and disillusionment piled a weight of suffering on shoulders too young to bear it. Couples like John and Carol would postpone having children.

Month by month, more and more people would be unemployed, half of them belonging to the lower middle class. Professionals, too, found their skills useless in the job market. Many hungry artists and writers had no security to speak of. John and Carol had two assets to carry them through the hard times: the small cottage at Pacific Grove where they could live rent-free, and the sea, from which they could gather food to eat and driftwood to keep warm. They were part of a group of young people—found everywhere—all poor, and all living the same way. Years later John recalled that time:

> We pooled our troubles, our money when we had some, our inventiveness and our pleasures. I remember it as a warm and friendly time. Only illness frightened us. You have to have money to be sick—or did then. And dentistry also was out of the question, with the result that my teeth went badly to pieces. Without dough you couldn't have a tooth filled. . . .
>
> Being without a job, I went on writing—

books, essays, short stories. Regularly they went out and just as regularly came back. Even if they had been good, they would have come back because publishers were hardest hit of all. When people are broke, the first things they give up are books. I couldn't even afford postage on the manuscripts.

Given the sea and the gardens, we did pretty well with a minimum of theft. We didn't have to steal much. Farmers and orchardists in the nearby countryside couldn't sell their crops. They gave us all the fruit and truck we could carry home. We used to go on walking trips carrying our gunny sacks. If we had a dollar, we could buy a live sheep, for two dollars a pig, but we had to slaughter them and carry them home on our backs, or camp beside them and eat them there. We even did that.

Keeping clean was a problem because soap cost money. For a time we washed our laundry with a soap made of pork fat, wood ashes and salt. It worked, but it took a lot of sunning to get the smell out of the sheets.

Steinbeck and Carol. This photo is thought to have been taken on their wedding day on January 14, 1930.

Carol had a strong sense of social responsibility. If things were wrong in the world you must act to right them. Not that John was insensitive to injustice. But it was Carol who brought him to the point of protest. She sympathized so strongly with the poor, the outcasts, the dispossessed. It was her sense of uncompromising morality that he liked, maybe because it echoed that quality in his mother.

John began working on a novel to be called *To a*

God Unknown. Its theme was man's relationship to the land. It would go through many revisions before publication. He shuttled back and forth between that writing and work on a group of short stories about California families. They dealt with how environmental changes influenced the way his characters lived. (The collection was never finished.) But it was as though he was anticipating the enormous impact of changes in the climate and economy of some large states.

Ted Miller offered to help find a publisher for one version of *To a God Unknown.* He began circulating it to editors who, one after another, turned it down. He was twenty-eight now, John told Ted, and he had to have at least one book a year out if he was to survive. But doubt gnawed at him. Could he do it? Did he still have to rely on his dad? Just in time to avoid disaster, Carol's father pitched in with a loan of several hundred dollars. But then the owner of their rented house in Eagle Rock, so nicely restored, decided to take it back as a wedding gift for his son. It meant moving from one miserable shack to another until they gave up trying to live near their friends and fled back to the family cottage in Pacific Grove, close to both sets of parents.

In 1930, the year he married Carol Henning, another event of great importance to John occurred. In a dentist's waiting room he met Edward Ricketts. He would become John's closest friend for nearly twenty years and the real-life model for key characters in several novels. John describes him as a small, rather slight man, but "capable of prodigies of strength and endurance."

Ricketts, born in Chicago in 1897, moved to California after university training as a marine biologist. He had opened a biological supply house called Pacific Biological Laboratories, located in Cannery Row in Monterey, when John met him. Already intrigued by marine life, John hit it off with Ed at first sight. Ed helped develop John's knowledge of this branch of science, and introduced him to the ideas of W. C. Allee, a pioneer thinker in the realm of ecology—the branch of biology that deals with the relationships between plants and animals and their environment.

The company provided live samples of marine creatures to high schools, universities, and medical research facilities. Ricketts conducted marine life research on his own, too, and used his findings in preparing scientific reports for publication.

Like John, Ed was interested in a multitude of things. They would sit for hours discussing political issues as well as scientific theories. Both loved hunting and fishing, and tinkering with engines of any kind.

John dropped by the lab frequently, watching Ed at his work and helping when he could. When the lab closed for the day, they would hang around the waterfront bars, gabbing with the fishermen and the winos.

With Ricketts's example, John found it easier to relax among people he hadn't known before. His ear, like a tape recorder, picked up their vivid talk. You can see the result when you read *Tortilla Flat*, *Cannery Row*, or *Sweet Thursday*.

Ricketts persuaded John that there were far greater similarities between animals and humans than people realized. Just as a biologist observes animal life, so a novelist could observe people's behavior and find comparable patterns. Ricketts believed that humankind does not stand above or outside the physical universe. It is an integral part of nature.

Not that John took everything Ricketts said as gospel. He gradually moved toward his own personal view of existence and the way we function in the world. In writings to come he would present characters whose thoughts, emotions, decisions, and acts are the product of complex processes, occurring within themselves and between themselves and others. In an essay about Ricketts written in 1951, after his friend's death, John said, "His mind had no horizons. He was interested in everything."

With the effects of the economic crisis spreading widely, Carol felt she must get a job. But she could find nothing steady, only odd jobs that lasted briefly and paid poorly. John worked steadily at his writing, holding visitors off till he quit in late afternoon. Then it was open house for anyone chancing to come by and share the little they had. On a lucky day there might be a gift of a thirty-five-cent gallon of red wine and maybe a loaf of sourdough. But no one grieved. They were all young, all sharing their troubles, pooling their meager resources. Special fun was dancing to the jazz of a wind-up phonograph.

The importance of Carol to John in these years can't be overstated. To a friend he wrote that, Carol "gets prettier all the time. I'm more in love with her

than I ever was. Sometimes I waken in the night with the horrible feeling that she is gone. I shouldn't want to live if she were." Steinbeck's biographer Jackson Benson holds, "Carol was important to Steinbeck the writer in a host of subtle ways. She pulled him up when he was down, revived him when he was out. As he got older Steinbeck tended to lose some of his ability to enjoy; occasionally, his sense of humor faded under the strain. Carol brought humor back to his consciousness; she wouldn't let him feel sorry for himself."

During much of 1931, John worked on a volume of interrelated short stories he would call *The Pastures of Heaven*. The characters in several were based upon people he knew, including his mother, and the setting was a valley like those in the Salinas region. Each story dealt with one family, but linking them was a newly arrived family whose unconscious evil wrecked the happiness of the others. He called them "tiny novels," with "no grand writing, nor any grand theme, but I love the stories very much."

It was a hard time for John and Carol. If they wanted to get away, their beat-up old Chevy wouldn't work, or they hadn't the money for gasoline. Then

there was rejection after rejection by publishers to whom Ted Miller sent John's work. He told Ted, "The haunting thought comes that perhaps I have been kidding myself all these years . . . that I have nothing to say and no art in saying nothing."

A lucky break changed everything. John learned of a new literary agency run by two young women, Mavis McIntosh and Elizabeth Otis, which handled Carl Wilhelmson's work. With Carl's letter of recommendation and Ted Miller's agreement, John sent them several of his short stories. They liked them so much that they agreed to represent him. For nearly forty years they not only sold his work but edited the manuscripts to make them ready for publication.

Elizabeth Otis became one of his closest friends. She respected his need for privacy when he became famous, and helped him with both professional and personal problems.

A publisher accepted *Pastures of Heaven* early in 1932—then went bankrupt. Luckily the editor who liked John's book moved to another firm, which agreed to issue it. Good news at last! Life looked even better when Ricketts hired Carol to work part-time as the lab's bookkeeper-secretary. She and John sometimes

joined Ricketts on collecting trips for the lab. Through Ed they met Francis Whitaker, a metal sculptor and a political radical. He tried—but failed—to swing John and Carol to a socialist point of view, and introduced them to people active in the farm-labor movement.

But Carol's job didn't last long; Ed couldn't afford to continue her fifty dollars a month pay.

John picked up an old manuscript, his novel *To a God Unknown*. He reworked it, making many changes till it looked like he had a new novel in hand. It is built around the central character of a rancher, something of a biblical patriarch, and is set in California country, using a drought as the chief plot device. A secondary plot deals with the inheritance of property or power by the coming generations. That theme would be vital to other works to come.

As they entered 1933, John and Carol felt they were heading for the rocks. The monthly check from his father wasn't enough to meet their expenses, and money was coming in from no other source. In March his mother suffered a massive stroke, causing almost total paralysis. His father lost heart for going on with life. John and Carol moved into the family home to help care for his mother. He was the only child free to do so, for by now the others all had their own families to care for.

He spent many hours every day at her bedside, helping nurses, receiving relatives and friends. For weeks he couldn't write. But when the doctors decided his mother would never recover, he turned to his writing again. His imagination turned back to his childhood, and he started work on a long story that would become part of *The Red Pony*. From now until the end of the summer of 1934, he would devote himself to short fiction, including the stories of *The Long Valley* and *Tortilla Flat*.

John's father collapsed in August 1933, remaining incapacitated for many months. The burden of economic worry and fear for his wife had been too much for him. John temporarily took over his father's work at the county treasurer's office. He had helped with office chores before this, and detested it. It was one of the most miserable times of his life—to stand by and watch both parents slowly going out. It felt like "slow torture," he said.

It was a grim time for the whole country. The Great Depression gripped America—and much of the world—all through the 1930s. At its cruelest depth in 1932–33, some 13 million Americans—one out of every four who had held jobs in 1929—were unemployed. The human misery implied by those figures is almost beyond belief. Immigrants by the thousands fled back to their old country. Young couples abandoned the hope of starting a family amid the ruin. One child of every five in New York City's public schools suffered from malnutrition. There were hunger riots in several big cities. Many people believed democracy might not survive. In Italy and Germany the economic crisis led to the collapse of governments and their replacement by the dictators Benito Mussolini and Adolf Hitler. Americans wondered: could that happen here?

But Franklin Delano Roosevelt had won the election of 1932, and as the new president he promised to help the forgotten man at the bottom of the economic pyramid. Poliomyelitis—the tragic crippling illness FDR had endured and surmounted—made many feel that, rich though he was, he could understand the suffering and poverty of those who struggled to make a living. He promised experimentation and change—what he termed a "New Deal."

FOUR

IT WAS BAD enough that millions of factory workers were losing their jobs year after year as the Depression worsened. But people throughout the country who made their living farming suffered intensely, too. Between 1929 and 1932 their net income fell by two-thirds. Prices dropped so low farmers didn't think it worthwhile to harvest the crops they had planted.

Then in America's Great Plains region something happened that made the suffering of farmers even worse. During and after World War I, through a belt of over one hundred counties, starting in Kansas and running into Texas and up into Canada, farmers lured west by quick profits had plowed submarginal land. Ample rainfall for a few decades had produced rich

A man and his sons walk toward a shack during a dust storm in the 1930s.

crops of wheat, but the rains stopped eventually and a terrible dryness set in. Late in 1931 a series of disastrous droughts and dust storms began. The topsoil blew away in huge clouds, darkening the skies, burying everything from houses and barns to fences and machinery.

The "black blizzard" cost the nation hundreds of millions of tons of soil and desolated thousands of families in the Great Plains states. Without the means to make a living, they took to the roads in search of work. Within the next five years, Dust Bowl farmers would desert the homesteads they or their pioneer ancestors had thought to root themselves in forever.

It was one of the worst environmental disasters in world history. The Dust Bowl covered big parts of Kansas, Oklahoma, Colorado, New Mexico, and the Texas Panhandle, and parts of Canada. For the farmers the economic crisis of the thirties and the ecological crisis only intensified each other. Farm families gave up all hope of making a living on the land. They moved west, first in a trickle, then in a flood. California! Land of promise? That was their goal, their hope of survival, their dream of prosperity.

This was not the first large migration west. Streams of migrants had been flowing west ever since the Gold

Rush of 1849. And the territory had welcomed them. Newcomers after 1849 came not for gold but for settlement. They saw in California a chance for economic betterment. By 1900 much of the state's empty land had been filled. And by 1930, as the Great Depression set in, the population reached 5.7 million. It had almost doubled in the last decade.

The people who fled the Great Plains states in the thirties and headed west were white, old-stock Protestants. About 300,000 of them climbed aboard their overloaded jalopies and traveled Route 66 to California. Although many came from states other than Oklahoma, they were all tagged as "Okies."

Hostilities were directed against the Okies, as well as striking farmworkers. The Okies were viciously attacked by many newspapers, by restrictive laws, and through cuts in relief funds. Not that California had welcomed all migrants in the past. Long before, Chinese, Japanese, Mexicans, and Hindus had entered the state to perform useful and needed work—building railroads, mining, harvesting—only to be persecuted, mobbed, lynched, restricted by legislation. But the state had never before tried to bar or mistreat migrants.

As that great migration poured into California,

Steinbeck was working on the first draft of the novel *Tortilla Flat*. He managed it somehow as his parents were wasting away. (His mother would die in 1934 and his father the next year.) Despite the gloom shadowing the Steinbeck family, the novel is full of fun. It is peopled with the Mexican migrants he worked with at the sugar mill as a young man. It is also based on experiences handed on to him by a friend, Susan Gregory, who'd taught Spanish in a Monterey high school. She got to know and love the community of Spanish-speaking people who lived on the edge of town. Her account of their songs and stories was excellent background for John's creation of his *paisano* characters. Anecdotes came, too, from the doctor treating John's mother and from Monterey's police chief. The novel's characters all had their real-life counterparts. What John achieved was the re-creation of a living community. He spoke of it as "light and I think amusing but true, although no one who doesn't know *paisanos* would ever believe it." For a book that seemed to be written so quickly and so easily, its quality would be astonishing.

Up to this time John had paid little attention to

the condition of farm labor in his state. The great central valley had become the heartland of farming, the richest industry in California. That multi-billion-dollar enterprise supplied a huge percentage of the fruit and vegetables Americans consumed: tomatoes, peanuts, melons, eggplants, raisins, peas, almonds, prunes, onions, potatoes, peaches, asparagus, lettuce, apples, plums, sugar beets, grapes—all this, and cotton, too.

The California farms were run like big factories. Most owners were not on the spot. They operated out of sleek offices in San Francisco, and they hired local managers to supervise the workers. Less than one-tenth of the farms produced over one-half of the crops. One farm owned by a single family covered 9,000 acres and in peak season gave hourly work to 1,800 people.

While Steinbeck was at work on *Tortilla Flat*—and short stories, too—strikes began to break out. They were not new in California. In 1933 nearly 50,000 farmworkers had taken part in strikes affecting almost all the major crops in the state. The next year saw another series of strikes in the fruit and vegetable fields. The workers were a mix of Mexican immigrants, Filipinos, Anglos, and some African Americans. In the Imperial

Valley, local and state police tear-gassed union meetings, forcibly evicted about 2,000 strikers and their families, and burned workers' homes. Many strike leaders were tried, convicted, and sentenced to jail terms. Steinbeck went to see them to find out what it was about. "I felt them, tasted them, lived them, studied them," he recalled many years later. All around him were the signs of mass suffering caused by the Great Depression. It was a time of intense labor struggles. Workers were desperate to defend the little that hard times had left them.

Wages for farmworkers dropped to the bottom. Starving farm laborers in California erupted in more than forty spontaneous strikes in the early thirties. The strikes were crushed almost at once by local authorities linked to the employers. Workers had no support from the traditional trade unions, which had concentrated on industrial workers and long ignored farm labor.

Late in 1932 the American Communist Party, seeking to recruit any and every worker, decided to fill the void by helping to organize the Cannery and Agricultural Workers Union. It sent in veteran organizers wherever protest erupted and recruited workers in the fields. Workers of all sorts were coming to see that they could best defend their own interests—securing decent wages, hours, and working conditions—by banding together in unions. And beyond this, they hoped that the American belief in freedom, equality, democracy, and justice for all, might one day be realized through a common effort.

The union made some headway with small gains in hourly wages. It broadened its reach through the support of liberals among middle-class people—writers, artists, lawyers, teachers, doctors. Among these friends of labor were people John knew. Francis Whitaker, the sculptor, was one. Through him, John and Carol met others who helped the union by raising money, writing leaflets, pamphlets, and newspaper articles, picketing, and giving speeches.

These new friends dropped in on the Steinbecks at their cottage in Pacific Grove. They talked excitedly about their experience defending labor. John shared their distrust of the corporations and the politicians. But unlike some, he had no faith in a revolution to get rid of capitalism. Challenged repeatedly to go out and see for himself what was going on, John decided he would.

One sign of his changing was "The Lonesome Vigilante," a new story. His first attempt to portray people caught in the labor turmoil, it was one of several stories John wrote in the summer of 1934. Gradually, his reputation grew as his stories were bought and published by various magazines, and finally collected in the volume, *The Long Valley* (1938).

Included in *The Long Valley* are four stories about the boy Jody Tiflin, tracing his development to manhood, and the meaning of that time of life. There is no continuous plotline; each story stands on its own. Yet grouped in *The Red Pony*, they fuse into a moving short novel. The reader, like Jody, comes to understand that life is always at risk. Our path from beginning to end goes through dangerous and unknown territory.

When *The Red Pony* was bought by the magazine *North American Review*, John was paid ninety dollars for it. "I didn't believe there was that much money in the world," he said. "The pure sparkling affluence of it went to my head for weeks. I couldn't bear to cash the check, but I did."

President Roosevelt was a dealmaker who understood how to make people work together. And he had a perfect partner in his wife Eleanor. She shared his energy and compassion. Roosevelt was unable to travel much because he had been crippled by polio, so Eleanor roved the country to find the facts and recommend the necessary action.

FDR asked Congress for broad executive powers and used them to wage war against the country's financial emergency. Congress swiftly passed bill after bill aimed at bringing about economic recovery. Federal relief for the hungry came first, and then billions of dollars to provide public projects—building dams, roads, bridges, parks—so that the unemployed could find jobs at last.

By November 1933, four million people were back at work. Farmers were helped with crop-control programs that raised farm prices, and their mortgage burden was lifted. It was a patchwork of plans improvised by the hour by lawyers, economists, and sociologists whom the New Deal brought into government service.

Workers were helped by a law that protected the

right to organize, and by the passage of the Social Security Act in 1935, which established unemployment insurance, social security, and low-cost housing by federal and wage and hour laws passed in 1938. Still, mass unemployment would persist throughout the 1930s.

It was in 1934 that a casual exchange between two men would have a deep and lasting influence upon John's work. Ben Abramson, owner of a Chicago bookshop, loved John's early published work and recommended it to his friend Pascal (Pat) Covici, head of a small publishing house, Covici-Friede. Covici immediately arranged to publish *Tortilla Flat* and several books that followed.

In the winter of 1934, Steinbeck met a young Okie active in the farmworkers' union. Cicil McKiddy, then twenty-four, was among the Dust Bowl migrants looking for farmwork. When a cotton strike broke out in the San Joaquin Valley in 1933, he helped the union and soon became secretary-treasurer of its local in Tulare. The strike began when cotton-picking wages were cut from one dollar to sixty cents per hundred pounds. After at least three strikers were killed by ranchers, the strike ended with a negotiated compromise, raising the wage to seventy-five cents per hundred pounds. That strike was a major struggle—the most successful for farm laborers before World War II.

After the strike, John pumped McKiddy for every detail about the conflict. He thought perhaps he could help the workers and at the same time gather material for his writing. He was especially interested in the history of Pat Chambers, a Communist and one of the strike leaders. He thought he could write about him in the first person, as though it were the autobiography of a radical labor organizer. Chambers and other strike leaders had been arrested under California's criminal syndicalism law, which was intended to cripple labor organization by charging union leaders with using force and violence and sending them to prison. The law was almost always on the growers' side.

Though John gathered facts about the life and work of migrant farm laborers, his use of the material was fictional. He avoided bringing in actual places and people, for he did not want to hurt anyone's feelings, he said. It is a composite valley he creates in the novel *In Dubious Battle*, as it is a composite strike.

In real life Pat Chambers and the other organizers faced terrible odds and took great risks in their devotion to labor's struggle for a decent life. But in John's novel they do not come off that way. The two main characters—Mac, the older leader, and Jim, his young apprentice—are concerned above everything else with using the workers and their strike for political purposes.

Steinbeck explained why he manipulates the reality in a letter to George Albee, which he wrote shortly before completing the novel and sending it off to his agent:

> I don't know how much I have got over, but I have used a small strike in an orchard valley as the symbol of man's eternal, bitter warfare with himself.
>
> I'm not interested in strike as means of raising men's wages, and I'm not interested in ranting about justice and oppression, mere outcroppings which indicate the condition. But man hates something in himself. He has been able to defeat every natural obstacle but himself

he cannot win over unless he kills every individual. And this self-hate which goes so closely in hand with self-love is what I wrote about. The book is brutal. I wanted to be merely a recording consciousness, judging nothing, simply putting down the thing. I think it has the thrust, almost crazy, that mobs have.

As Jackson Benson put it, "If Steinbeck's organizers are cold, it is because the author was cold." He didn't take sides in the novel. It is neither for nor against labor.

Meanwhile Carol was working many hours a day typing his manuscript. He couldn't do it himself because "my typing is so very lousy." Carol had recently been hired by the State Emergency Relief Administration, where she put in a full day, and then came home to do John's typing.

John wrote his first draft by pencil. (Later he would switch to using a pen.) He would fuss over both the kind of paper to write on and the pencil to use. When he tried a new brand of pencil and it proved better, he'd be elated. If worse, he'd be mad. His handwriting was so minute it was terribly hard to read. No wonder it wore on poor Carol. Later, the staff of his publisher, Viking, would take over the handscript and do the typing. (This, of course, was long before the word processor came into use.)

A modest author, he did not brag about the quality of his writing, but liked to tell people about the quantity. "I am capable of a tremendous amount of work," he told a friend. "I have just finished a novel of 120,000 words, three drafts in a little over four months."

He warned his agent Mavis McIntosh that the strike novel was "a brutal book, more brutal because there is no author's moral point of view," and went on to say his use of working people's language might "seem a little bit racy to ladies clubs." She offered it to Pat Covici, who agreed to publish it.

Steinbeck anticipated criticism from both the political left and right. The left held a vision of an ideal communist who could do no evil. The right saw only a damnable radical who could do no good. "Neither side," he said, "is willing to suspect that the communist is a human, subject to the weakness of humans and to the greatnesses of humans."

In May 1935, Covici-Friede published *Tortilla Flat*.

From this time on, Steinbeck would never have to worry about money. Nor was he ignored as just another hopeful writer.

Reviews of the novel were favorable, and the book became a best seller. Critics thought it a good folk-flavored comedy with warm, likable characters. This surprised him. "Curious that this second-rate novel, written for relaxation, should cause this fuss," he said. "People are actually taking it seriously." He was dismayed when the Commonwealth Club of California awarded the book its gold medal as the best California novel of the year. John said he felt very bad about it, and refused to go to the awards ceremony. "This is the first and God willing the last prize I shall ever win," he wrote a friend. Soon royalty checks began coming in. And with their first chunk of cash John and Carol took off for Mexico on a vacation that lasted more than three months.

Just before they left, the *San Francisco Chronicle* ran an interview with John which described him as "of giant height, sunburned, with fair hair and fair mustache and eyes the blue of the Pacific on a sunny day, and a deep, quiet, slow voice." He would later do his best to avoid such interviews.

In November came the news that Paramount had bought the film rights to the novel for four thousand dollars. That was at least four times more money than he had ever earned before from his writing. Many millions of Americans at that time earned only one thousand dollars a year, which was considered a decent income.

Soon after returning from Mexico, the Steinbecks bought a small lot at Los Gatos, north of Monterey. They designed their own plans for a new house that a local contractor would build for them.

Meanwhile, in Pacific Grove, John worked on a new story that would become *Of Mice and Men*, his most popular short novel. The book's title comes from a poem by Robert Burns, "To a Mouse," written in 1785:

The best-laid schemes o' mice an' men
Gang aft a-gley;
An' lea'e us nought but grief and pain,
For promis'd joy.

He had meant it to be a children's book, but it turned out differently. By May 1936 he had a good part of it in hand, when Toby, his new puppy, chewed it into scraps. "The poor little fellow may have been acting critically," he said. He had to write it all over again.

Of Mice and Men is the story of Lennie and George, two men wandering the country with the dream of some day settling peacefully on their own land. Lennie, a powerful, but semi-retarded man, is looked after affectionately by George. The novella is set on the ranch where they find temporary work, sharing the bunkhouse with others. Inevitably it ends tragically, revealing through Steinbeck's superb eye for significant detail his deep sympathy for the victims of the Depression thirties.

The Steinbecks moved into their new house in July. Carol was relieved to have John more to herself. She had thought he spent too much time with Ed Ricketts and the gang around the lab. John was pleased with his new study, designed by himself: a small room with a bed, an oak desk, a gun rack, and a little bookcase. It was a happy time, working on his tale of the two migrants, George and Lennie. He finished the book in August and sent it to Elizabeth

Otis, telling her he didn't expect it to sell very well. Pat Covici, more optimistic, took it on, and scheduled it for publication early in 1937.

Then came another of those unforeseen happenings that can make a huge difference in one's life. An editor for the *San Francisco News* who'd liked *In Dubious Battle* very much visited John to ask if he'd write a series of articles for the paper on California's migrant farmworkers. The assignment meant tackling the kind of investigative journalism that can change the way a serious social problem is understood and dealt with.

Yes, said John, I'll do it.

FIVE

STEINBECK OF COURSE knew something of the condition of migrant workers long before the *News* approached him. Now, accepting the challenging assignment, his first move in late August of 1936 was to go to San Francisco to discuss the project with *News* editors, and to meet with federal officials of the Resettlement Administration (RA) there.

The RA was the only government agency—state or federal—created to try to do something to help the migrants. In 1935 the RA had set a goal of building a chain of permanent government-supervised camps for the migrants. But opposition to the project from a conservative majority in Congress cut the project down to a limited number of "demonstration" camps.

The aim of the RA was to prove such camps

worked, in the hope that growers and local governments would construct their own camps on the RA model. That goal was up against a wall of indifference or hostility. The public either didn't know how bad conditions were for the migrants, or was indifferent. The political power of the growers was so great at every level of government that most officials turned a blind eye to the migrants' plight, or even cooperated with vigilantes in crushing efforts to organize the migrants.

John would travel to the San Joaquin Valley to observe the migrants' living and working conditions, both in their ramshackle squatters' camps and in the RA's camps. He would be accompanied by Eric Thomsen, a manager of the RA program. Wanting to be noticed as little as possible, John bought an old truck and outfitted it with blankets, cooking equipment, and some food.

The men headed south, stopping first at some squatters' camps. John had seen hobo camps ("jungles," they were called) before, but what he saw now was far worse. As he approached a squatters' camp, he wrote, it looked like a city dump, "a litter of dirty rags

Opposite: Makeshift homes belonging to Okies, 1936.

and scrap iron, of houses built of weeds, of flattened cans or of paper." A man might earn four hundred dollars a year at most, if he was lucky enough to make every harvest. But if his jalopy broke down, or he missed some harvests, he'd have to feed his whole family on maybe one hundred and fifty dollars a year. Looking into the faces of such men and women, John saw deep fear of starvation threatening everyone in the camp.

John described several migrant families he met:

> There is more filth here. The tent is full of flies clinging to the apple box that is the dinner table, buzzing about the foul clothes of the children, particularly the baby, who has not been bathed or cleaned for several days.

The family has been on the road longer than the builder of the paper house. There is no toilet here, but there is a clump of willows nearby where human feces lie exposed to the flies—the same flies that are in the tent.

Two weeks ago there was another child, a four year old boy. For a few weeks they had noticed that he was kind of lackadaisical, that his eyes had been feverish.

They had given him the best place in the bed, between father and mother. But one night he went into convulsions and died, and the next morning the coroner's wagon took him away. It was one step down.

They knew pretty well that it was a diet of fresh fruit, beans and little else that caused his death. He had had no milk for months. With his death there came a change of mind in this family. The father and mother now feel that paralyzed dullness with which the mind protects itself against too much sorrow and too much pain. . . .

This is a family of six; a man, his wife and four children. They live in a tent the color of the ground. Rot has set in on the canvas so that the flaps and the sides hang in tatters and are held together with bits of rusty baling wire. There is one bed in the family and that is a big tick lying on the ground inside the tent.

They have one quilt and a piece of canvas for bedding. The sleeping arrangement is clever. Mother and father lie down together and two children lie between them. Then, heading the other way, the other two children lie, the littler ones. If the mother and father sleep with their legs spread wide, there is room for the legs of the children.

If John had been wondering what the subject would be for the big book he hoped next to write, then this journey through near-hell gave him the signal he needed. What would help him above all was a friendship that began when he met Tom Collins, manager of the RA camp at Arvin, in Kern County, in the southern part of the Central Valley. Collins would become John's chief source for accurate information about the migrants.

John described Collins as "a little man in a damp,

frayed white suit. The crowding people looked at him all the time. Just stood and looked at him. He had a small mustache, his graying, black hair stood up on his head like the quills of a frightened porcupine, and his large, dark eyes, tired beyond sleepiness, the kind of tired that won't let you sleep even if you have time and a bed."

Collins, about forty, was a Catholic who once intended to be a priest. He set the model for how a camp should be run. His democratic spirit inspired the two thousand campers, who made their own rules for living here, and saw that they were carried out.

John stayed a week at Arvin, looking, listening, asking questions, making notes every night on what he saw and heard, the gossip, the folklore. Adding to his own observations were copies of the biweekly reports Collins sent to the RA headquarters in Washington. Richly detailed, they proved invaluable for his *News* articles, and later, for the writing of *The Grapes of Wrath*.

Traveling through the Central Valley, John stopped at Salinas, where a squatters' camp had grown up on the borders of his hometown. He found it a terrible situation. A band of local vigilantes, armed with clubs and rifles, had forced lettuce workers to give up their strike, while the police sat by and watched.

Another stop was made at the RA camp at Gridley, near the state capital at Sacramento. Because word of John's reporting expedition had spread around the state, the camp manager warned him to be very careful. His photograph was being circulated (probably by the Associated Farmers) with a warning that this man could make trouble for the growers.

His visits to the RA camps brought John to certain conclusions:

From the first, the intent of the management has been to restore the dignity and decency that had been kicked out of the migrants by their intolerable mode of life.

In this series the word "dignity" has been used several times. It has been used not as some attitude of self-importance, but simply as a register of a man's responsibility to the community.

A man herded about, surrounded by armed guards, starved and forced to live in filth loses his dignity; that is, he loses his valid position in regard to society, and consequently his whole ethics toward society. Nothing is a better example of this than the prison, where the men are reduced to no dignity and where crimes and infractions of rule are constant.

We regard this destruction of dignity, then, as one of the most regrettable results of the migrant's life, since it does reduce his responsibility and does make him a sullen outcast who will strike at our Government in any way that occurs to him.

The example at Arvin adds weight to such a conviction. The people in the camp are encouraged to govern themselves, and they have responded with simple and workable democracy. . . .

As experiments in natural and democratic self-government these camps are unique in the United States.

As for the people in power who opposed any attempts to help the migrants, John had this to say:

The Associated Farmers, which presumes to speak for the farms of California and which is made up of such earth stained toilers as chain banks, public utilities, railroad companies and those huge corporations called land companies, this financial organization in the face of the crisis is conducting Americanism meetings and bawling about reds and foreign agitators. It has been invariably true in the past that when such a close knit financial group as the Associated Farmers becomes excited about our ancient liberties and foreign agitators, some one is about to lose something.

A wage cut has invariably followed such a campaign of pure Americanism. And of course any resentment of such a wage cut is set down as the work of foreign agitators. Anyway that is the Associated Farmers contribution to the hunger of the men and women who harvest their crops.

Upon his return home, John wrote Tom Collins to thank him "for one of the very fine experiences of a life. I hope I can be of some kind of help." And he enclosed a check for the migrants' use. He added he'd try to get people to donate books for the migrant kids whose schooling was so uprooted.

The articles sat on the *News* editor's desk for a while because, as Steinbeck wrote his agent, "The labor situation is so tense just now that the *News* is scared stiff to print the series. Any reference to labor except as dirty dogs is not printed by the big press out here. There are riots in Salinas and killings in the streets of that dear little town where I was born."

But the paper soon mustered the courage to run John's articles. They appeared in the *San Francisco News* October 5 to 12, 1936, under the heading, "The Harvest Gypsies."

John was by no means through with that story. . . .

The new year—1937—began with trumpets blowing for John's short book, *Of Mice and Men*. The Book-of-the-Month Club chose it, assuring a large readership. It hit the best-seller lists quickly. Within a few weeks 117,000 copies were sold. Reviews were mostly positive, though not wildly enthusiastic. Yet great numbers of readers found the story so warm, so compassionate, the characters so real, the dialogue so true, that new editions kept coming out.

With decent income assured, John and Carol added more furniture to their new house and welcomed guests. Both Ed Ricketts and Tom Collins dropped in often, as did neighbors and old Stanford classmates. The talk was usually political: what FDR's New Dealers were doing about the economic crisis, whether a revolution—as in Soviet Russia—might be in the offing, talk eased by lots of cheap wine.

Steinbeck was besieged by requests for interviews, book signings, lectures, autographs. Always shy of publicity, he complained the ballyhoo was driving him nuts.

Now John and Carol had the means to escape the frenzy. Married seven years, they decided to carry out their dream of a long vacation abroad. That spring they took a freighter via the Panama Canal to the East Coast where they spent a couple of weeks in New York. Pat Covici welcomed them and insisted John submit to the usual publicity projects for launching a new book: press conferences, interviews, book signings, cocktail parties. Drinking too much, John quarreled with Carol, who withdrew and lost herself in liquor.

It was a bad time that threatened their marriage. Seeing relief in a change of scene, they tried to put aside their grievances with one another, and in June sailed for Scandinavia. They stopped first in Sweden and then went on to Denmark and Finland. They met other writers, tried out restaurants and cafés, and visited with the foreign publishers of Steinbeck's works. Their last stopping place was the Soviet Union, then going through the trials the dictator Josef Stalin had rigged against people he wanted to get rid of. His secret police forced people to give false confessions of working against Stalin, and he then had them executed. John had thought he might like to write a novel about that country, probing what group life was like under communism. He would return some ten years later for another look.

Returning to New York on a small freighter, John went to work on his dramatization of the novel *Of Mice and Men*. He had no experience in writing for the stage, yet he had a very good ear for dialogue. With the help of the eminent playwright and director George S. Kaufman, the script was readied for production.

The play opened on Broadway on November 23,

1937. Steinbeck was not in the audience. To everyone's amazement, he had chosen instead to leave with Carol for California before rehearsals had started. The play was a big hit, with film companies bidding for the rights to make a movie of it. James Cagney, one of Hollywood's biggest stars, wanted to play George. The Drama Critics Circle gave it the award for the best play of the season.

Before leaving the East, he stopped in Washington, where he met with an official of the Farm Security Administration (the successor to the RA). John told him he planned to write a novel about the migrant workers. He meant it to be an honest, realistic portrait of how those people lived. It would be a great help, he said, if the FSA would assign Tom Collins to help him for a few weeks of research. Agreed.

John bought a Chevrolet for the trip home. First the Steinbecks headed for Chicago to see Ben Abramson, the bookdealer who'd led Covici to John, then west along Route 66, the highway the Okies followed to reach California.

Although Carol said later that John took no notes along the way, his description of a migrant family's passage on Route 66 is so vividly detailed in *The Grapes of Wrath* you'd think he worked from film footage. It's an example of how an artist's extraordinary memory may serve him.

Back home, John prepared for his research trip, tuning up the old truck he'd used before. He met Collins at the new FSA camp in Gridley, which Tom was now managing. John figured it would take three weeks to gather the information he would need for his novel. They roamed the state from Stockton to Needles, stopping wherever migrants gathered to seek work.

Again, John took notes, interviewing a great many of the migrant workers and drawing from Collins's many stories of his long experience in the field. Collins would serve as the model for Jim Rawley, the fictional manager of the "Weedpatch" government camp in *The Grapes of Wrath*.

By November 7, John was home again. A friend remarked how tired he was, so down, too. One wonders, was it because the big book he was aiming for now looked like more than he could handle? Writers often slip from an upbeat mood to bouts of depression when they feel maybe they can't get to the guts of the story.

From New York, reports kept coming in of how much audiences loved *Of Mice and Men*. It led the playwright Jack Kirkland to ask, and obtain, John's permission to dramatize *Tortilla Flat*. But it turned out Kirkland had no feel for the *paisano* style of life, and the play was a flop, closing after four performances.

That didn't short-circuit John's popularity. Hollywood dangled enticing offers for him to come write for this producer or that. And at the other extreme, destitute people—strangers—wrote begging him to send money, for food, for rent, for medical treatment. It was heartbreaking, but how could he navigate in that vast sea of misery? Which appeals merited help?

Organizations with solutions to the world's problems begged for the use of his name on their letterhead, plus some cash. He would always be generous. But he couldn't turn himself into a philanthropic agency if he meant to keep on writing.

An unexpected and distressing aspect of such public success was the damage it did to friendships. Some of his college friends, themselves writers still struggling to make good, resented John's success. They grew jealous, angry, and the friendships disintegrated.

The worst effect was the fraying of his marriage.

Carol had given up everything for his career. She, too, was talented, wrote prose and poetry, painted, drew caricatures. Yet she not only carried out all the tedious chores of their households, but spent endless hours helping him with typing and editing, and comforting him when he was down on his luck. She was also a rigorous commentator on the work in progress. Now he had everything, and she, what? Not even the children one might have expected. Once, a few years earlier, she had turned to another man for solace, but that relationship went nowhere. And when John learned of it, he felt terrible.

As winter came on, he continued to make field trips to the migrants. In February of 1938, with Tom Collins, he visited two camps in Tulare County, flooded by many days of rain. His anguished reaction is conveyed in this letter sent to his agent, Elizabeth Otis:

> I must go over into the interior valleys. There are about five thousand families starving to death over there, not just hungry but actually starving. The government is trying to feed them and get medical attention to them with the fascist group of utilities and banks and

huge growers sabotaging the thing all along the line and yelling for a balanced budget.

In one tent there are twenty people quarantined for smallpox and two of the women are to have babies in that tent this week. I've tied into the thing from the first and I must get down there and see it and see if I can't do something to help knock these murderers on the heads. Do you know what they're afraid of? They think that if these people are allowed to live in camps with proper sanitary facilities, they will organize and that is the bugbear of the large landowner and the corporation farmer. The states and counties will give them nothing because they are outsiders. But the crops of any part of this state could not be harvested without these outsiders. I'm pretty mad about it. No word of this outside because when I have finished my job the jolly old associated farmers will be after my scalp again.

He did more than look at trouble. He helped. Day after day, without sleep, coughing badly, he pulled half-starving people into makeshift shelters from the torrent of rain. The migrants were too weak from lack of food to help themselves.

At the end of the month he went home, staying briefly, then heading back to the migrant camps. This time it was with a photographer on assignment from *Life*, the hugely popular picture magazine. If their millions of readers learned about the horror of the migrant camps, maybe something would be done about them.

He wouldn't take money for his work; it was to go for relief instead. "The suffering is too great for me to cash in on it," he wrote Elizabeth Otis. But *Life*, for reasons unknown, did not publish the Steinbeck picture story on the migrants' conditions. Instead, after *The Grapes of Wrath* was published and had become a sensational best seller, the photographs were used to illustrate an article on the book and another about the movie made from the book.

It was at this time that Steinbeck met a superb documentary filmmaker. Pare Lorentz had earned great praise for his film *The Plow That Broke the Plains*, the story of the Dust Bowl, a production subsidized by the New Deal government. Conservatives attacked it as a "liberal" project the government should not have supported.

Lorentz and Steinbeck hit it off at once. Lorentz tried to get editors he knew to take the article John had written for *Life*. But they backed off.

John's anguished report on the flood-besieged migrants of Tulare Country finally found print. The *Monterey Trader* published it in its April 15, 1938, issue, calling it "Starvation Under the Orange Trees." Friends of the migrants, organized in the Simon J. Lubin Society, obtained John's permission to reprint his 1936 articles on the migrants, plus "Starvation Under the Orange Trees," in a pamphlet, with photos taken by Dorothea Lange. She was an FSA photographer whose pictures of migrant workers in the West and South had won great praise. One of her pictures, a migrant mother with a child at her breast, was chosen for the cover. It became a classic photograph, reproduced more often than almost any other one as the decades have gone by. Called *Their Blood Is Strong*, the twenty-five-cent pamphlet went far and wide, was reprinted many times, and earned enough to keep the society's work going.

The Lubin Society supported all efforts to organize the migrant workers. The Congress of Industrial Organizations (CIO) aimed specifically at winning union representation for them, and launched the United Cannery, Agricultural, Packing, and Allied Workers of America in 1937. Asked to help raise money for migrant relief, John lent his name to the "John Steinbeck Committee to Aid Agricultural Organization." The group would be active in the struggles ahead.

SIX

JOHN'S FIRST PLAN in dealing with the migrant worker experience was to write a satirical novel. In "L'Affaire Lettuceberg," he focused on the vigilantes and their brutal acts during the Salinas lettuce strike. By the end of April he had scribbled 60,000 words— only to be disgusted with the result. He told Pat that his aim was to help people understand each other. Yet out of him had come a draft he feared would cause hatred.

This wasn't the big book he had dreamt of. As satire it was a failure. Carol read it and agreed. Taking her advice, he threw the manuscript into a bonfire.

He took up another of the ledgers he used for his first drafts in longhand. It was now the middle of May, 1938. He was determined to write an epic this time, to create a legendary migrant family alive to every reader. While working on the novel, he kept a journal, writing in it each day before he picked up the thread of the novel. In a way, the journal resembles the letters he used to write friends in earlier times, as warm-ups for the creative work.

This diary of a novel, with one hundred entries, runs from May 31 to October 26, 1938. It was published long after, in 1989, as *Working Days: The Journal of "The Grapes of Wrath."* For anyone who wants to be a writer, it is an invaluable book.

He began the novel with a clear sense of how he'd shape it. The narrative centers on a large family as it heads west, hoping for a better life in California. The Joad family represents the thousands of Dust Bowl families. In his journal Steinbeck keeps telling himself how urgent it is to get right "the detailed description of the family I am to live with for four months. Must take time in the description, detail, looks, clothes, gestures. Ma very important. Uncle John important. Pa very. Got to take it slowly. I don't care how long it is. We have to know these people. Know their looks and their nature." Alternating with the chapters on the Joads are brief chapters exploring the economic and historical factors that led to the migration.

Steinbeck had a large collection of recorded classical music. He would select pieces to be played just before he began to write, or during a break in his work. Tchaikovsky's *Swan Lake* ballet music and Stravinsky's *Symphony of Psalms* were especially good to set the mood or the rhythm he wanted.

Right from the beginning he knew how he wanted the story to end. It would be a scene in which the young woman Rose of Sharon, who has just had a miscarriage, offers her breast milk to a starving man.

The novel is full of superbly drawn characters: Tom Joad first of all, the fierce protector of the family; his mother, Ma Joad, a tower of strength in the most harrowing moments; Pa Joad, broken by the loss of his farm; Jim Casy, the former preacher, who weaves the moral thread of the story and gives his life for the workers' movement to organize.

And then of course Tom's younger brothers and sisters, so real in their hopes, confusions, dreams. There are a dozen other characters—strangers met on the road or in the migrant camps—and every one drawn to life and essential to our appreciation of the world the novel creates.

In the course of the novel we come to understand how the migrant families are shaped into a community, with each person's life woven into the values and dreams of them all.

Telling the story is a nameless narrator, conscious of all the issues confronting the migrants, the growers, the government. He stands with the poor and the oppressed. The narrative voice shifts from gritty to lyrical, from cool to raging anger, always carrying us along.

While he worked, friends continued to visit the Steinbecks at Los Gatos. But they quickly realized John's mind was elsewhere, in the world of his novel, not with them. His journal shows how intense was his need to create people as real as he was. Sometimes he felt terribly lost if the work wasn't going well.

Their neighborhood had become so popular that new houses were rising all around them, shattering the peace and quiet they wanted. For ten thousand dollars they bought fifty acres of land five miles north of Los Gatos and that September began building a new house there.

Bad news broke just then: Pat Covici's publishing firm had gone bankrupt. Luckily, Pat was able to extricate himself and move into a larger publishing company, The Viking Press, as a senior editor. Viking would publish all of Steinbeck's work from that time on. With him, Pat had taken John's short story collection *The Long Valley*, which Viking published in September 1939. The sales got off to a great start.

What to call the new novel? What title would be best? It was Carol who came up with the right one. "The Grapes of Wrath," she said. It's right there in your manuscript. And she pointed out the passage:

> . . . in the eyes of the hungry there is a growing wrath. In the souls of the people the grapes of wrath are filling and growing heavy, growing heavy for the vintage.

Those lines had emerged in John's mind. He must have remembered them from the first stanza of the great "Battle Hymn of the Republic," composed by Julia Ward Howe:

Mine eyes have seen the glory of the coming of the Lord;

He is trampling out the vintage where the grapes of wrath are stored;

He hath loosed the fateful lightning of his terrible swift sword;

His truth is marching on.

Written in 1861, and sung to the tune of "John Brown's Body," it inspired Lincoln's armies as they marched into battle to crush the forces of slavery.

On October 26, 1938, John finished the novel. It had taken him only forty-three working days over a five-month period to write the 260,000 words. A scholar who studied the original manuscript found that Steinbeck wrote so minutely on the ledger sheets that he used only one hundred and sixty-six of them to complete the manuscript of the novel. You can envision how tiny his writing was when you realize the first edition of the novel ran to six hundred and nineteen printed pages. Poor Carol probably needed to use a magnifying glass when she did the arduous job of typing up the manuscript. Viking rushed it to press, and it reached the public in February 1939.

By now *The Long Valley* was appearing on the best-seller lists, and the reviews were hot enough to make any writer joyful. One critic held that "a genuinely great American writer" was on his way. Another said the stories were a remarkable collection from a writer who never repeated himself nor was guilty of a single sloppy sentence.

John would rarely write short stories in the future. It was the long narrative that gave him the room he needed to develop character.

In January of 1939 the Steinbecks moved into their new house. Worn out by the intense work on the novel, and suffering from the pain of neuritis, an inflammation of the nerves, John flopped into bed. When Elizabeth Otis came west to go over the editorial changes Viking was asking for, she thought he looked like an old man, although he was only thirty-seven. She tried to get him to delete obscenities in the dialogue, for fear bookstores might refuse to carry the book. He gave in to some changes, reluctantly. Viking also wanted him to change the ending, where Rose of Sharon offers her breast to a starving man. But he'd have none of that.

He believed his ending was exactly right. The passage stayed in.

When Elizabeth told him Viking was planning a large first printing, he told her they shouldn't. "It will not be a popular book." His warning was ignored. And a good thing. By publication the advance sale was ninety thousand copies.

That month John was elected to the American Academy of Arts and Letters, a highly valued honor. Adding to good news was the purchase of film rights to *Of Mice and Men* by Lewis Milestone, one of Hollywood's finest directors. And then another Hollywood man dropped in to introduce himself and launch a lasting friendship. It was the great master of comedy, Charlie Chaplin. He lived nearby.

Not all the news was good. John heard of rumors spreading that he was a dangerous radical, a "Red," a communist. And that the FBI was investigating him, asking others all sorts of questions about his life, his habits, his friends, his opinions. He figured the Associated Farmers—the organization of the big growers in California—must be behind all this. Was his Americanism questioned because he undertook themes of social and economic justice?

He was warned by friends to be careful of where he went, whom he met with, what they said. He knew dirty tricks had been played on labor organizers, throwing them into jail or subjecting them to vigilante violence. It was even hinted an attempt might be made upon his life.

He was scared. Who wouldn't be? Was this the price of fame?

When Steinbeck received the first copy of *The Grapes of Wrath*, he was immensely pleased with its look and feel. As he had requested, Viking placed "The Battle Hymn of the Republic"—the words and music—on the endpapers of the novel.

The book was dedicated "To Carol who willed it, to Tom who lived it."

Soon reviews began pouring in. Most were highly favorable, although some critics wondered what the last chapter meant, and others wished he had not included those general chapters in between the narrative chapters. In 1940 the book won the Pulitzer Prize, and John gave the one-thousand-dollar award to a younger writer friend.

Of all Steinbeck's works of fiction, *The Grapes of*

Wrath became the anchor of his fame. It brought the thirty-seven-year-old writer great praise—and angry denunciation. Praise was often voiced for the powerful narrative of the Joad family as representative of all the Okies in their struggle to survive. Like the Okies, readers, too, learn the lesson of the importance of cooperation to achieve a common purpose.

But not everyone liked it. Congressman Lyle Boren of Oklahoma, one of the Dust Bowl states, charged the book was "a lie, a black, infernal creation of a twisted, distorted mind." It was said it promoted hatred of class against class. Yet the literary critic Stanley Edgar Hyman wrote that "as a careful reading makes clear, the central message of *The Grapes* is an appeal to the owning class to behave, to become enlightened, rather than to the working class to change its own condition." The book was banned as subversive by numerous libraries. Yet it contains a defense of private property and private enterprise, even while denouncing the big landed interests for their irresponsible treatment of the migrant workers.

The novel ignited a national explosion of indignation over the plight of the Okies. The huge publicity around the novel, rather than delighting Steinbeck, upset him. He feared so much public attention could be destructive. Now the reading public expected him to repeat the work he'd done. It felt like everybody wanted to hear from him. His mail was flooded with requests for him to give speeches. It made him terribly self-conscious. "I simply cannot write books," he said, "if a consciousness of self is thrust upon me."

One of the leading book critics, Louis Kronenberger, wrote that "No novel of our day has been written out of a more genuine humanity, and none, I think, is better calculated to awaken the humanity of others." Many compared the book in its public impact with Harriet Beecher Stowe's *Uncle Tom's Cabin*, the anti-slavery novel of pre–Civil War time.

The book's sales shot way up and have stayed high for an uncommonly long time, right up to the present day. It has sold many millions of copies since its publication nearly seventy years ago, and has been translated into many languages. It soon became required reading in schools, colleges, and universities.

By happy coincidence, Ed Ricketts had a book of his own published around the same time as John's,

called *Between Pacific Tides*. It had taken years to research and write and would become an important
sourcebook for the study of marine life on the Pacific
Coast. John and Ed began talking of a joint research
project that might lead to their collaboration on a
book.

Meanwhile another project was about to be
launched. Pare Lorentz, the documentary filmmaker,
asked John to work with him on a movie about public
health, to be called *The Fight for Life*. It was President
Roosevelt's idea. He hoped such a film would gain public support for a comprehensive public health bill he
wanted to place before Congress.

The film would be based upon Dr. Paul de Kruif's
research into the hazards of childbirth and ways to reduce the rate of infant mortality. John met Lorentz and
his staff in Chicago in late April, staying for a month.
Together they looked into how a medical center func-
tioned in a poverty-stricken neighborhood. Lorentz
meant to show the need to fight against the poverty
and ignorance blocking the path to medical progress.

Again, as he had when learning about migrant
workers, John interviewed a wide variety of people,

including doctors and then the patients, to determine how poverty affected their health and what such a center meant in their lives. It was a year when John's own health became a concern. Neuritis caused him almost crippling pain with an inflamed leg. But he believed strongly in what he was doing and wouldn't drop out. When the film crew came to Hollywood to shoot some interior scenes, John would join them for a week or two at a time.

By midsummer, *Grapes* had sold over 200,000 copies and was a number one best seller. The movie rights went for $75,000, a top price at the time. During his working periods in Hollywood, John often saw his childhood friend, Max Wagner. Max and others in his family worked in film production.

While in Hollywood, John made arrangements with Lewis Milestone, director for *Of Mice and Men*, and the scriptwriter, Eugene Solow, to review the script. Looking it over, he said it was fine, but then went over it with pencil in hand. And when he was finished, said Solow, the voice you heard was Steinbeck's and no one else's.

Of Mice and Men was filmed mostly in the San

Fernando Valley, and John visited the locations a few times. When editing was done, they screened the movie for him. He liked it very much.

In Hollywood John talked with Nunnally Johnson, one of the best screenwriters, who was preparing the screenplay for *Grapes*. John found that everyone working on the movie was deeply moved by the novel and devoted to making an honest film from it. John knew that a novel and a film are very different forms of expression, and trusted Johnson to do it justice in that medium.

To help achieve that goal, he had Twentieth Century-Fox, the producers, hire Tom Collins for $15,000, as technical adviser. He knew Tom would insist on accuracy of look and feel and tone as the director, John Ford, shot portions of the film in and out of government camps. Tom was pleased with the outcome, and so was John, who wrote Elizabeth Otis after a preview that, "No punches were pulled . . . it is a harsher thing than the book, by far. It seems unbelievable but it is true."

Late that summer of 1939, Carol walked out on John. The tensions between them had become unbearable. A big source of trouble was conflict over family life. Carol wanted to have a child, and John said no. Once she became pregnant, he insisted on an abortion. He feared that a father's responsibilities would interfere with his writing. Reading his diaries, you see how uncertain he was of his writing, and his ability not only to keep at it but to make it the best. It seems John never appreciated all that Carol was doing for him. He took her sacrifices for granted.

Later, in a letter to a friend, he said: "I must face it. I am not good at marriage. I find that I am a lousy husband and that is something I might as well accept since I do not think I will change at my time of life." He wrote Elizabeth Otis that he was to blame for the troubled marriage; he was the one who was failing to make it work. Seeking comfort, he went down to Ed Ricketts's place to stay for a while.

The separation was brief. Carol had been so sick of his behavior that she thought she couldn't take it any longer. Yet very soon back she came. Trying to restore some warmth to the marriage and to get away from the pressures of the book and the movie, John and Carol drove up to the Pacific Northwest, where peaceful landscapes might ease their spirits.

During those last months of 1939 the threat of another world war dominated the news and everyone's mood. One after another, independent nations—Spain, Albania, Austria, Czechoslovakia, Ethiopia, China—had fallen victim to war and fascism. And now, two great powers—Germany and Japan—seemed on the brink of launching wars of aggression against their neighbors. Should the worst happen, could the United States stay out of it?

In September, Nazi Germany invaded Poland, launching World War II. Still, most Americans hoped they'd stay out of it, and went on with the routine of daily life. Keeping on the go, the Steinbecks flew to Chicago, where John met with Pare Lorentz and Paul de Kruif to complete work on the documentary film. Friends noticed that the couple would sometimes let down their guard and say or do outrageous things to hurt one another.

It must have been hard for John to calm down when attacks on *The Grapes of Wrath* continued into 1940. The book remained on the best-seller lists despite the fact that nothing so powerful and true in its depiction of working-class life had won such popularity before. The book was denounced as filthy, outrageous, untruthful. Worse, Steinbeck himself was called all sorts of nasty names. One rumor planted in the press held that the migrants themselves hated him for lying about them.

Running counter to the attacks on the novel was a new book, *Factories in the Fields*, by Carey McWilliams, director of California's Division of Immigration and Housing. A socioeconomic study, it documented much of what Steinbeck had depicted in his novel. McWilliams said the California's growers knew of "the inconvenience and misery, the hardship and suffering, which is implicit in the system itself. But they sense, even if they will not willingly admit, that a readjustment of the system would involve a readjustment of the entire agricultural economy. Hence they are driven to defend the system and its consequences much as slaveowners were driven to defend chattel slavery."

Backing for the book's truthfulness came, too, from Eleanor Roosevelt. The president's wife visited the migrant camps in spring 1940 and told the press that nothing in *The Grapes of Wrath* was exaggerated.

But the strongest support for Steinbeck came out of hearings held in 1939–40 by the Senate Committee on Education and Labor, chaired by Senator Robert M. LaFollette. Its official report in 1940 detailed the "shocking degree of human misery" among farmworkers and exposed the violent tactics used by the Associated Farmers in its openly admitted policy of taking the law into its own hands.

In reaction to pressure from both sides, Steinbeck turned away from the creation of fiction and took refuge in the study of science.

SEVEN

WHEN *THE GRAPES OF WRATH* dropped off the best-seller lists, Steinbeck was relieved. He had had enough of the unforeseen byproducts of success and celebrity. He'd rather be collecting specimens of wildlife from the sea than creating fictional characters.

Spending his weekends at Pacific Grove, on weekdays he worked with Ed Ricketts at the lab. His investment had made him a half-owner of the lab. "The world is sick now," he wrote his friend Sheffield. "There are things in the tide pools easier to understand than Stalinist, Hitlerite, Democrats, capitalist confusion and voodoo. So I'm going to those things which are relatively more lasting to find a basic new picture."

He began intensive study of marine biology, helped Ed with the lab work, and made several field trips with him in the Bay area. Soon he was emerging from the mood of despair, writing Elizabeth Otis, "I can't tell you what all this means to me, in happiness and energy. I was washed up and now I'm alive again, with work to be done and worth doing."

Notes he made in this period suggest the point of view he was developing. He believed there was a "creative association between observer and object." The observer has a point of view. It conditions how he sees what he is examining. It is a sort of creative interchange. The observer's expectations—shaped by his life, his experience—affect how he sees the object. What peephole is the observer looking through, Steinbeck wanted to know.

He believed that "the life of any individual is closely bound up in the material and social life of his city, with its climate, its water supply, its swamp or altitude, its politics, factories, its food supply and transportation; so is the life of each individual in the tidepool inextricably relative and related to every surrounding environmental factor."

Later, after one of their field trips, he said, "We knew that what we would see and record and construct would be warped, as all knowledge patterns are warped, first, by the collective pressure and stream of our time and race, second by the thrust of our individual personalities."

These ideas would help shape the fiction to come, as well as the journal of the exploratory marine expedition he planned with Ed Ricketts. Late in March 1940, John and Ed were ready for their month in the Gulf of California. John, paying for the voyage, handled all the preparations, buying equipment and supplies and obtaining necessary permits from the State Department and Mexico.

Going aboard with John and Ed were the ship's captain, a crew of three, and Carol serving as cook. As they left Monterey on their seventy-six-foot boat, *Western Flyer*, they saw the threatening signs of war: navy planes and ships, gathering for action someday.

Steinbeck spoke of the trip as a research project for Ricketts. But it was more for himself. He was looking for fresh material to write about, not the tragedies of human existence, but the microscopic life of marine animals.

The object of the voyage was to collect and preserve

marine invertebrates along the seashore. Out of it came *The Sea of Cortez* (the older name for the Gulf of California), a journal in which Steinbeck records his basic beliefs at that time. He does it in a leisurely way, punctuated by humor. He enjoyed the technique of collecting specimens, comparing it to how he gathered the bits and pieces of human experience for creating his fiction. He thought it would be a "darned fine book" though not one the public would be eager for.

Back at the ranch, John wondered what he'd do next. Covici hoped he'd take up work on another novel. But he was sick of the clamorous response to *Grapes*, the mad mixture of the greatest praise and the most scurrilous abuse. What about the movies? A documentary film, as solid and useful as *The Fight for Life*? Hollywood producers were offering him big money to write scripts for feature films. What he much preferred was a proposal by Herbert Kline for a film about the struggle to provide decent medical care for the people in a Mexican village.

He plunged into the project, financing it with his money and funds from friends. He took on the job of producer as well as scriptwriter, and then went down to Mexico with Kline and Carol. The village of Patzcuaro was chosen as the site for filming, and research began among the local people. The outcome was a script (to be called *The Forgotten Village*) that balanced the villagers' belief in the healing power of the local witch doctor with the struggle to secure a water source cleansed of the microbes that caused so much sickness.

With the script completed, and shooting not to begin till late fall, John and Carol flew to Washington. He hoped to arouse interest in the film among officials concerned with U.S.-Mexican relations.

While in the capital, he managed to secure a brief meeting with President Roosevelt. John suggested that a propaganda office be set up using print, the visual media, and radio, to combat the propaganda of Nazi Germany in the Western Hemisphere. Although the United States was not yet in the war, it turned out the government was already preparing for it.

At home, the Steinbecks were in domestic trouble. The marriage was falling apart rapidly. John had been introduced to Gwyndolyn Conger, a jazz singer, in a San Francisco nightclub, and she and John took to meeting secretly. He was thirty-seven and she was twenty when they met. They liked each other very much, but the strain of a double life was hard to bear. That winter John fell sick again and again. Somehow he managed to do some work on *The Sea of Cortez*, and began making notes about *paisano* life in Monterey that would later be useful in writing *Cannery Row*.

Though it made little sense in this strange and deeply troubling time, he bought a small house in Monterey, which he and Carol moved to. He still felt love for her, and feared to hurt her. It was on his conscience that the aftermath of her abortion had left her sterile. And her physical condition, like his, had been gradually worsening.

He sensed that Carol had begun to suspect he was carrying on an affair with another woman, and one day he told her about Gwyn. That ended it. In April 1940, Carol left him for good. John felt torn up by the roots, he told Elizabeth Otis. Only continuing with his work kept him from going crazy. "God knows I'm no bargain," he said. "Probably as difficult to live with as anyone in the world. . . . I hope Carol can find peace somewhere. She can't with me."

Carol moved to New York, fleeing the wreck of

their marriage. John sold the Los Gatos ranch, and hired a man to cook and clean for him in Monterey. A lucky diversion came when Lewis Milestone, the director, told John he'd raised the money to film *The Red Pony*. Soon he arrived to work with John on the script, as they'd done so successfully with *Of Mice and Men*.

It seems Carol wasn't happy in New York, and decided to return to California to be near her old friends. John then determined to try living in New York, as he once had, so long ago. It may have been a passing mood, but it turned out to be a permanent change. Both friends and literary critics later thought the move was a mistake. John was never meant to be a New Yorker. His best work, they contended, was rooted in California. Many people, after *The Grapes of Wrath*, mistakenly pigeonholed him as a political radical and a social realist in his writing. But his temperament led him to try new ventures, new ways of seeing life, new ways of writing about it.

Before moving, he talked to Gwyn, sounding her out on their future. She agreed to marry him when his divorce came through. In the autumn of 1941 he and

Gwyn moved into a hotel in Manhattan. They would marry in 1943.

Meanwhile John began to write material, refusing payment, for the government's Foreign Information Service. He traveled frequently between New York and Washington, where he met many European refugees who told him of their experience under Nazi rule. Now forty, he was not subject to the draft, but he wanted to do whatever he could to help the war effort.

Out of the dramatic and horrifying stories he'd heard from the refugees in Washington, he began to shape the novel that would be called *The Moon Is Down*. He joked that this was done on assignment from a government agency. It began in his mind as a play and evolved into the novel. It tells the story of an unnamed Nazi-occupied country and the people who organize to resist it.

John's first draft, however, had set the action in an American town occupied by the Germans. He meant to show that we, too, could have people among us willing to collaborate with an occupying power, while others would risk their lives to oppose it. The aim was to make clear to Americans "it *could* happen here." But the government disappointed him when

UP CLOSE: JOHN STEINBECK

it disapproved of that approach, deeming it defeatist. Nevertheless, he went ahead with the book, making the setting any country.

Then everything changed, for everybody. On December 7, 1941, Japanese naval and air forces made a surprise attack on the U.S. Naval base at Pearl Harbor, Hawaii. They sank twelve U.S. warships, destroyed about 170 planes, and killed almost 2,500 Americans. The U.S. Congress declared war on Japan, Germany, and Italy.

Soon after Pearl Harbor, *The Moon Is Down* was ready to meet the public in several forms, as novel, as play, as movie. The book leaped onto the best-seller lists, with a million copies sold in the first year. Film rights went for $300,000, four times the amount paid for *The Grapes of Wrath*. Soon the novel appeared in several foreign translations, too.

The play opened on Broadway in April 1942. Drama critics didn't think much of it; it ran for only nine weeks. But it was successful on a road tour, and a hit in Stockholm and London. Audiences responded to the theme of solidarity—a call for people to stand firm against oppression and in defense of freedom and democracy.

The Steinbecks' divorce came through in 1943. John married Gwyn in March 1943 and they moved out of Manhattan and into a rented house at Sneden's Landing in Rockland County, an easy distance from New York. John continued to write broadcasts for the government, wiring the texts down to Washington. Still, he disliked being only on the fringe of the war. He wanted to be much closer to the action. His chance came when the Air Force asked him to write a book for the public about how bomber crews were chosen and trained.

He would move from air base to air base in the United States, living with the crews as they trained. Should that project work out well, he would then fly overseas with them and describe them in combat.

A huge task, he thought, and he would give it his best. In Washington the air command introduced him to a photographer assigned to work with him. The two men began their sweep around the country to air bases—Arizona, Colorado, Florida, Illinois, Texas. They got to fly on every kind of plane, sat in classes with the air cadets, shared their meals, slept in their barracks. The trip was tiring. His rounds completed in late June, John had about five weeks to write the book for delivery on August 1.

He met that deadline by dictating the book into a recording machine. He reeled off four thousand words a day, worried that it couldn't be much good at that speed. But it was—a fine example of the best journalism, and evidence of his intense interest in how community life is shaped.

Called *Bombs Away: The Story of a Bomber Team,* the book sold widely and was bought by a film producer for $250,000. John, rich enough by his standards, handed the money to the Air Force Aid Society Trust Fund. He didn't think he should profit by his work for the war effort.

The film company wanted him in California while production was getting under way. In September he and Gwyn moved to Sherman Oaks in the San Fernando Valley, only to find the studio so chaotic that nothing was being done. The film was never made. Instead, he pitched in when an old friend, Jack Wagner, asked him to co-author a small movie called *A Medal for Benny.* They did it in three weeks. Not out until 1945, the movie is long forgotten.

A better job was his work on *Lifeboat,* a movie about the survivors of a sunken ship, drifting on the sea in a lifeboat. It was John's idea, bought by

Twentieth Century-Fox, and assigned to the director Alfred Hitchcock. With his usual speed, John wrote the script in a month, and then he and Gwyn moved back to New York.

They found a small apartment in the lower half of a brownstone on East Fifty-First Street in Manhattan. It had a small garden in back, which he could cultivate himself. Although he and Gwyn were only recently married, it looked like they'd soon be separated by the war. John had long been hoping some newspaper would send him overseas to report on the war. The *New York Herald Tribune* agreed to it, if he would get the necessary approval from the government. In spite of all he had already done for the war, right-wing groups warned that he was a dangerous radical. But attacks on John were brushed aside by the War Department. When Gwyn learned he was going abroad, leaving her alone, she was furious. He couldn't understand why she would object to his serving in the war in the only way open to a man of his age. It was a bad start to their marriage.

It was June 1943 when Steinbeck boarded a troopship bound for Britain. He would be gone nearly five months, moving with the American forces from Eng-

Steinbeck with his friend Max Wagner, probably in London, 1943.

land to North Africa and then to Italy. His dispatches were phoned to the *Herald Tribune* and then relayed to a syndicate of many other papers, both in the states and abroad. (A selection of them was published in 1958, long after the war, and called *Once There Was a War.*)

Working alongside other reporters, he found them to be "a curious, crazy and yet responsible crew." He felt like a tourist among all those professionals. He learned to censor himself. No criticism of anyone in the service, from the buck privates to the commanding generals. That didn't mean he lied. He just left out things, or the censors cut them out.

There are many passages in *Once There Was a War* you linger over. Here is just one, written from Italy on October 6, 1943. He tells us civilians at home read in the papers of war plans and practices, but not some of the things the reporter really saw:

He might have seen the splash of dirt and dust that is a shell burst, and a small Italian girl in the street with her stomach blown out, and he might have seen an American soldier standing over a twitching body, crying. He probably saw many dead mules, lying on their sides, reduced to pulp. He saw the wreckage of houses, with torn beds hanging like shreds out of the spilled hole in a plaster wall.

There were red carts and the stalled vehicles of refugees who did not get away.

The stretcher-bearers come back from the lines, walking in off step, so that the burden will not be jounced too much, and the blood dripping from the canvas, brother and enemy in the stretchers, so long as they are hurt. And the walking wounded coming back with shattered arms and bandaged heads, the walking wounded struggling painfully to the rear.

While still on the Italian front, he speculates about why ex-soldiers refuse to talk about their experience in combat. He traces in detail what the body and mind go through in battle, and how when the soldier survives, what happened to him becomes dreamlike, and then day by day slips completely out of memory. "Perhaps all experience which is beyond bearing is that way," he concludes. Not really true. Psychiatrists treating victims of combat found its horrors could do lasting damage.

He returned to New York on a troopship in mid-October, suffering from the effects of those months on the battlegrounds. His memory failed him for a time, and his hearing, too, was damaged. He was so depressed his friends worried about him.

Gwyn, too, was depressed, still unable to forgive him for deserting her right after their marriage and subjecting her to all those months alone living in constant fear he might be killed. His sister, too, agreed that he had come back a different man. The war had changed him, and not for the better. The spirit of fun, the playfulness, had been knocked out of him.

In January, *Lifeboat*, the movie he had scripted, appeared in the nation's theaters. It got four-star reviews, but Steinbeck was so enraged by what was added—slurs on organized labor, and the racist depiction of an African American seaman—that he tried, but failed, to have his name removed from the screen credits.

As winter came on, he and Gwyn left for a vacation in Mexico. They moved around the tourist sites, with John holing up each day for a few hours to work on *The Pearl*, a Mexican tale about Kino, a young fisherman who finds a fabulous pearl. He had picked up the story years before during the Sea of Cortez expedition. The outcome was a short, lyrical narrative, almost like a scenario for a film. (A movie was made of it in 1947.) Musical themes were used to help convey the range of emotion Steinbeck wanted the reader to feel. What comes across is that our lives are shaped by forces we may not even be aware of. For we are each of us but a single unit within a larger organism—the family, the village, the ethnic group, the tribe, the nation. And that larger organism struggles with other large organisms—for position, for power, for control, for profit. What the outcome may be for the individual, we can only guess at.

Before going overseas, John had written his Stanford friend, Webster Street, that "after the war is done I want about ten acres near the ocean and near Monterey and I want a shabby comfortable house and room for animals, maybe a horse, and some dogs and I want some babies. . . . And I'm pretty sure it's what Gwyn wants too." He added that he thought his earning years were about over, but "we'll get along. There's love in the house."

Gwyn wanted children, too, and now a baby was on its way. On August 2 their son Thom was born. "An exciting time," John wrote a friend. "Thom seems to be a baby-shaped baby and I like him very much. He just eats and sleeps, but I can think of worse kids." A month later the family of three had moved to Monterey, where John had bought an old adobe house close by the waterfront that he would hire a crew to remodel for them.

Now he seemed happy—back with his old friends, Ed Ricketts and the Monterey people, and his sisters, Mary, Esther, and Beth. They hoped he'd come home for good. John had Ed read the draft of *Cannery Row*, a new novel he'd been working on. How would Ed take the character called Doc, John's fictional portrait of Ed? Ricketts read it, saw himself portrayed as a mythical hero, and said only, let it be published as it stands. It's written in kindness.

The novel asks fundamental questions. What are the most important things in our lives? How shall we live? Accept death? Do we make room for love?

But as the months passed, nothing worked out for John, except for the warmth of his reunion with Ricketts. Some his other friends turned cool or distant. They thought his success and wealth had changed him. Quarrels broke out and people dropped away. Monterey's business and political conservatives were openly hostile because of his support of migrant labor. His own bleak moods and drinking didn't help. Too much alcohol could make him act like a clown. Once, out dancing with Gwyn, doing the tango, he flopped right over her, landing them both on the floor.

EIGHT

CANNERY ROW WAS published in January 1945 and sold very well. Huge numbers of fans would buy anything Steinbeck wrote. The novel was a nostalgic return to prewar times, an affectionate tribute to a community and friends he'd loved. There is no tightly woven plot, only a series of linked anecdotes about men and women he depicts charmingly, and the places where they hung out.

He said he had written it for soldiers who asked him to "write something funny that isn't about the war. . . . We're sick of war."

Among the thirty-two chapters are many parties. Mixed with the fun is the collecting of specimens for Doc's biological lab. Doc himself is a friendly character, yet a solitary figure who suffers loneliness.

The novel took what John called "a pounding" by the critics. Steinbeck was just by, one said; this wasn't up to the high stand his earlier work. Conservatives disliked it as an ment of materialistic values, of money grubbing meanness. Yet the book has proved to be one of most popular, a memorable evocation of that wa front community.

Take this lyrical passage on the day's beginning:

Early morning is a time of magic in Cannery Row. In the gray time after the light has come and before the sun has risen, the Row seems to hang suspended out of time in a silvery light. The street lights go out, and the weeds are a brilliant green. The corrugated iron of the canneries glows with the pearly lucence of platinum or old pewter. No automobiles are running then. The street is silent of progress and business. And the rush and drag of the waves can be heard as they splash in among the piles of the canneries. It is a time of great peace, a deserted time, a little era of rest.

Cats drip over the fences and slither like syrup over the ground to look for fish heads. Silent early morning dogs parade majestically picking and choosing judiciously whereon to pee. The sea gulls come flapping in to sit on the cannery roofs to await the day of refuse. They sit on the roof peaks shoulder to shoulder. From the rocks near the Hopkins Marine Station comes the barking of sea lions like the baying of hounds. The air is cool and fresh. In the back gardens the gophers push up the morning mounds of fresh damp earth and they creep out and drag flowers into their holes. Very few people are about, just enough to make it seem more deserted than it is.

Now John picked up *The Pearl*, completing a draft of the short novel quickly. Then down to Mexico to work on a shooting script of the film version with its Mexican director, Emilio Fernandez. Leaving baby Thom with John's sister Beth, Gwyn joined him for a month to help by researching folk music. When they returned to Monterey, Steinbeck again felt rejected

by everyone but Ed Ricketts. He began to think he must break this isolation by returning to New York and the many friends he now had in the big city.

Meanwhile, there was more work to be done on *The Pearl*, both the novel and the film, and with the whole family he returned to Mexico. In April 1945 President Roosevelt died. John felt it as a personal loss, for he had come to love the man, as did so many people during the Great Depression. On May 8, Nazi Germany surrendered to the Allies. The war in Europe was over. The war in Asia would end with the Japanese surrender on August 14. The Steinbecks stayed on in Mexico because an exciting new project was proposed to him by a film production company. Would he write a screenplay about the life of Emiliano Zapata, a Mexican revolutionary who lived from around 1879 to 1919? He was a savior to the Indian peasants, and even while he lived, a legendary figure. John was delighted with the offer. He liked writing about great historical figures whose heroism needed remembering.

Gwyn had been taking Spanish lessons, and she was able to help John begin his research in Mexican archives. As though he hadn't more than enough to

Steinbeck with Gwyn, Thom, and Willie the dog, in Cuernavaca, Mexico, 1945.

busy him, he also began making notes for a big novel, *The Wayward Bus*. News of that must have pleased Covici and John's agents, for it was years since he had tackled a large-scale work.

That September, John decided to give up California, selling the Monterey house. It was no longer where his heart was. He bought two adjacent brownstones on East Seventy-Eighth Street in Manhattan. There was a garden in back, a prime reason for his choice. And they could rent out one of the houses, a good investment as real estate prices soared with the ending of the war.

In October, Gwyn was pregnant again. When John went back to Mexico for the filming of *The Pearl*, she joined him there, leaving Thom with a nursemaid. But he was so intensely busy she felt left out. Angry over his neglect, she flew back alone to New York. Superb as he was in portraying characters in his fiction, sometimes he seemed unable to understand how badly his behavior affected others, including family.

Work on shooting *The Pearl* dragged on. It wasn't completed until December. When John came home, he saw that Gwyn's pregnancy was proving difficult and painful. They had to live helter-skelter till the extensive remodeling on their new home was completed. Even before that was done, John set up a workroom in the basement, and tore into *The Wayward Bus*. Originally he'd thought of it as the story of a Don Quixote in Mexico. But he soon realized that wouldn't work, and changed the locale to California.

When remodeling of the two Manhattan houses was completed, John rented the second one to Nathaniel Benchley and his wife Margery. Nat, much younger than John, was a *Newsweek* staffer but soon switched to freelancing, writing biographies and children's books. The two couples became intimate friends for the three years they would be close neighbors.

Recalling those years, Nat said there was "a lot of the little boy left in him, if by little boy you can mean a searching interest in anything new, a desire to do or to find or to invent some sort of diversion, a fascination with any gadget of any sort whatsoever, and the ability to be entertained by comparative trivia." Steinbeck often visited a neighborhood toy store to rummage through the stock, once buying a cap pistol as a Valentine's day present for his wife.

"One of the most glorious facets of his character," Nat said, "was his humor . . . not gag-type humor, but . . . the result of his wildly imaginative mind." After the daily measure of writing (one thousand words per day was the goal) he often turned from art to carpentry or some other task. He redesigned a toilet and rebuilt it, he fixed his fishbowl, he made a birdcage, he invented a tool rack which he built himself. It's "amazing," he said, "how many things there are to do in a house, new or old."

Steinbeck liked to read poetry, late at night, with a good friend and a good drink beside him. More than once, said Nat, while reading aloud Petrarch's sonnets voicing the poet's love for a woman, John would weep, unable to read through to the end.

John loved the big city. He delighted in the abundance of fine food, the best theatre, the best music. Now he added jazz to his enthusiasms, reading up on its history, collecting recordings, and meeting many musicians. He and Eddie Condon, the great guitarist, would jive for hours about favorite musicians, and when Condon opened his own jazz club in Greenwich Village, John and Nat went down often to hear the combos.

He was learning to be a father, too. He had a lot of fun playing with his first son, Thom. On June 12, 1946, the Steinbeck's second son, named John, was born. Mother and child did not do well for some time. It didn't help the strained marriage when Steinbeck took to working on his novel away from home, at the Viking office. His intense concentration on his work—and himself—made it hard for him to adjust to parenthood. And soon he was gone a month when summoned down to Mexico to solve problems with the final stages of *The Pearl*.

Home again, he completed a draft of *The Wayward*

Bus. Was it a good book? He had no idea. This time he worked by dictating the story into the machine in an expressionless voice, then had the dictation typed up so that he could make revisions on the page. He felt uneasy about the draft, speaking of it defensively. Yes, it was what he wanted to say, he told a friend, and it was there if you wanted to find it.

In mid-October the Steinbecks parked their children with a nanny and left for a month's vacation in Scandinavia and France. Everywhere they went John was besieged by reporters and photographers. In the bookstores every morning he autographed his works for crowds of excited fans. In Norway he was awarded the King Haakon Liberty Cross for *The Moon Is Down*, an honor hitherto given only to heroes of the Norwegian anti-Nazi resistance movement.

With the spotlight always focused on John, Gwyn was upset. She felt people treated her as though she were invisible. When she worried about being away from the boys so long, they cut the trip short by a week.

Home again, John began working on a play about a modern Joan of Arc confronting a world threatened by atomic bombs. After a few months he gave up on it.

In February 1947, as John turned forty-five, *The Way-ward Bus* was published. The advance sales were huge, nearly a million copies. It meant a lot of money. But he wanted more than money. The reviews, what were they like? Contradictory. One said "fine," another, "thin," and so on. It depressed him. Maybe he ought never to read reviews; they only canceled each other out.

And deeply disturbing was their family life. He and Gwyn were disagreeing about almost everything. Friends thought Gwyn was deceitful, not to be trusted. There were rumors that she had affairs with other men. She had hoped for a career in the music world, but that ambition was frustrated. His needs always came first. His writing, that was everything. Her talent? Ignored. Her place was to keep house, care for the kids, and admire her husband's achievements. As for friends, he had a great many, and admirers flocking around him wherever he was. No wonder she was jealous. Then, too, there was the considerable difference in age, each finding it hard to understand the other's needs and moods. If they weren't quarreling, they were giving each other the silent treatment. The Benchleys thought the conflict was so basic it couldn't be overcome. After one of their fights, Gwyn fled to California with the boys, but returned in a month when John flew out there and begged her forgiveness.

Then—one more quarrel—and he felt he'd had enough. He accepted an offer from the *New York Herald Tribune* to report what was going on in Russia. The trip would be taken with Robert Capa, a photographer John had met while reporting on the war in Europe. Capa had earned an international reputation for his courage and artistry in covering the Spanish Civil War in the 1930s and then World War II. The plan was for him to photograph Russians in their everyday life, while John commented in his journal on what they saw and learned.

This was shortly after the Russians had played a huge role, and at a tremendous cost in lives, in the defeat of Nazi Germany. Relations between the U.S.A. and its wartime ally were friendly at this time. Capa believed the Russian people, despite their communist regime, were like people anywhere. It was this human side he wanted to capture in words and pictures.

They planned to fly to France first, stay awhile, then go on to Russia. Gwyn insisted on leaving the boys with their nanny so she could go along on the first leg of the trip. They were stunned to find on arrival in Paris that John was greeted with the same wild enthusiasm as a year before in Scandinavia. A new French edition of *The Grapes of Wrath*—fifty thousand copies!—was issued just as they arrived. It was a happy reversal of the cool critical reception John's last novel had just received back home.

In mid-July Gwyn returned to New York and the children while Steinbeck and Capa flew to Moscow. John had visited Moscow ten years before. This time he felt progress had been made, at least in what he could see—new buildings, cleaner streets, better-dressed and healthier-looking people. The people they met, including many of the leading Russian writers, had endless questions about life in America. The answers John gave were of course filtered through official translators, well aware of what could and could not be said. And as for translating Russian responses to American questions, the same. If any Russian had something critical to say of his own society, he'd better think twice.

What did come through was Russian fear of an American attack. The Cold War was just getting under way, with each side wary of the other, and each fearful of another war. After World War II ended, the world was divided into two armed and hostile camps. They stood for different social and political systems. One was composed of nations allied to or occupied by the Soviet Union; the other, a looser network of states, was led by the United States. This rivalry was called the "Cold War" because it generated a dangerous arms race and armed conflicts in several parts of the world. No one then could have predicted that the U.S.S.R. would cease to exist as a communist dictatorship in 1991.

Steinbeck's reporting of what he saw was superb. Especially vivid was his portrait of Stalingrad, the city almost totally destroyed by the German army, yet which managed to turn the tide against Hitler.

On leaving Russia, John and Capa visited Prague and Budapest briefly before returning home. John had been feeling homesick for some time. When Gwyn wrote she'd acquired a Connecticut farm near the sea for their summer use, he replied it would be great for the boys to learn how to handle boats.

In September John and Capa were back in New

York. John told a friend he hoped to complete work quickly on a book based on their Russian visit, for he wanted to devote all his time to writing a big novel he'd been thinking about for a long time. (It would be called *East of Eden*.) Perhaps he was reacting to the critics who'd been putting him down for limiting himself to small projects all these years, instead of creating another novel as large and significant as *The Grapes of Wrath*. He thought he'd go out to California soon to get close to the material he'd need for the new book.

Gwyn did not welcome him with open arms on his return from Russia. And as he gave all his attention to completing the book, she fell sick. John had to take care of the kids while trying to write, and it proved too much. Nat Benchley observed that he simply didn't know how to handle the constant racket made by little boys.

In January he left home and family and flew to California, where he rented a cottage near Monterey. He visited scenes from his past, absorbing the tone, the color he'd need for his novel. He found that Lewis Milestone had just finished filming *The Red Pony*, and was ready to work on the film of *Cannery Row*.

Gathering impressions made him feel he could pull off the big book. It meant so much to him he didn't care if it took the rest of his life. He had to make it good, and he had to make it unique. He wouldn't rush it, he wrote Pat Covici, for "it's the whole nasty bloody lovely history of the world, that's what it is with no boundaries except my own abilities."

Mixed with exciting research for the new book was the delight he felt in being close to Ed Ricketts again. They partied with friends, and as in the old days went out together to collect marine specimens. Steinbeck was having such a great time he wondered if it had been a mistake to move to New York. He decided that in the summer he would put aside work on the novel and join Ed in an expedition off the coast of British Columbia.

Reluctantly, he returned to his family in New York. Both his and Gwyn's medical problems hospitalized them briefly. They got better, but the marriage was as shaky as ever. Nothing, it seemed, could bring them any closer.

And then early in May, Steinbeck got terrible news. Ed Ricketts had been crossing railroad tracks when a train struck his car, severely injuring him. John flew instantly to California to comfort his dearest friend. But it was too late. Ricketts had just died.

Steinbeck was stunned. His marriage was shattered, and now he had lost the friend he loved more than anyone else. He stayed in Monterey to settle what to do with Ed's belongings. The only thing he kept for himself was the microscope they'd used on the Sea of Cortez expedition. He would always remember Ed as a great man and teacher. "No one who knew him will deny the force and influence of Ed Ricketts. Everyone near him was influenced by him deeply and permanently. Some he taught how to think, others how to see or hear. Children on the beach he taught how to look for and find beautiful animals in worlds they had not suspected were there at all. He taught everyone without seeming to."

A few days later he was back in New York, to be told by Gwyn there was no point in dragging things out. She wanted a divorce, now. It was hardly a surprise, but hard to handle coming on top of Ed's sudden death. He packed some bags, including the manuscripts of unfinished projects, and moved into a hotel. The boys, kissing their father good-bye, must have been utterly confused. What was going on?

Steinbeck—scared, sad, lost—wrote friends seeking comfort and support. Gwyn took the boys to California to spend the summer with her mother. John's friend Elia Kazan tried to help by having John join him in Mexico for more research on the *Viva Zapata* film. He flew down to Mexico again and again over the next several months.

In October 1948 the divorce became final. In December Steinbeck was elected to the American Academy of Arts and Letters, a great honor. But this did not serve to pull him out of a deep depression. The only thing that helped lift his spirits was Gwyn's promise that Thom and John would spend the next summer with him.

Steinbeck had enough information on Zapata now to start writing the screenplay. He had done extensive homework for it, digging into university archives and reading everything he could find on Mexico's life in that revolutionary decade of 1910 to 1919.

His work on the Zapata story occupied him during the winter and into spring of 1949. He missed his sons badly, and in April flew from Mexico to New York for a week. He saw the boys every day, taking them to the Bronx Zoo or on walks in Central Park.

Then he was back in California to check out his script with the producer, Darryl Zanuck. It was now that through mutual friends he met the woman who would become his third wife. She was Elaine Anderson Scott, who'd studied drama production at the University of Texas, where she'd met and married the actor Zachary Scott. When she was introduced to Steinbeck, her thirteen-year marriage was pretty much over.

That encounter was a great turning point in the life of John Steinbeck.

NINE

IT DIDN'T TAKE long for John to fall in love. Elaine was a tall, attractive woman, bright and outgoing, and so capable that she had become stage manager for the Theatre Guild, a major production company in New York, a rare achievement for a woman in those days. She had moved to Hollywood when her husband was given a film contract by the Warner studio and had quickly climbed to stardom. But their marriage, like the Steinbecks', had gone on the rocks. Steinbeck liked her immensely, and they dated often. He needed a wife who could help him break free of these last desolate years. They would be married in December 1950.

He turned in a draft of the Zapata script and picked up his notes for *East of Eden*. During two summer months, his sons joined him for a happy time fishing and boating and hiking. Steinbeck felt his creative energy flooding back and his ability to work renewed. He planned to make use of true elements of his family history and meld it with what his imagination conjured up; a sort of treasure chest for his sons to discover when they came of age.

But the fun was mixed with pain. He recognized that his son Thom was "in trouble in some way. I

Steinbeck and Elaine at the Frankfurt, Germany, airport.

only know it because I feel it in his eyes and in the quick frantic and quickly covered emotion of yesterday. I don't know what to do but I know I must do something to help him. He has become silent and Gwyn says defiant." Sometimes Thom refused to go to school, Gwyn reported, claiming he'd missed the bus. When the boys came to stay with John and Elaine overnight, he sensed Thom was "in some deep emotional trouble. I could feel it. And I am pretty sure it is a simple feeling of rejection, of *not* being loved." Elaine began to tutor Thom whenever they were together, and it seemed to help.

Taking his boys along, John and Elaine would often summer on the island of Nantucket, the old whaling port off the coast of Massachusetts. Elaine and the boys spent the days on the beach, while John stayed home, writing, until early afternoon when he joined them for swimming and sailing in their own small boats.

That fall of 1951, with Elaine and her teenage daughter Waverly he moved to Manhattan, into a brownstone he bought on East Seventy-Second Street. Because reviews of his work these last years had not been very favorable, he felt shaky about the novel in progress. He leaned heavily on Pat Covici for help and reassurance. But if Covici criticized him, he got upset, even angry. Nevertheless, he completed the big novel in early November, nine months after he'd begun it.

Steinbeck built *East of Eden* on the mythic pattern of the Old Testament narrative in Genesis—the Cain and Abel story. He reworked the story of the brothers through three generations of the Trask family, with Caleb and Aron representing Cain and Abel.

But much of the book offers a factual account of Steinbeck's own maternal family, the Hamiltons. The Hamilton family is mixed in with the fictional family, the Trasks, and it is they who are really at the heart of the novel. The result, as one critic put it, is "a huge grab bag."

The draft of the novel ran to 265,000 words—the longest and hardest work he'd ever done. Of course there was much rewriting to be done, a necessary process but one he didn't relish tackling.

He worked on *East of Eden*, from January 29 to November 1, 1951. Before beginning each day's session, he wrote a work diary in the form of a letter to Pat Covici. He kept to this every working day till the first draft of the novel was finished. It was a method he'd used earlier, when working on *The Grapes of Wrath*. Call it a trial run, or a warm-up exercise. Of course later he revised the draft of the novel extensively—far more, perhaps, than he cared to have his readers or his critics know.

These unmailed letters were handwritten on the left-hand pages of the notebooks, with the facing pages holding the day's work on the novel. Published in 1969 (a year after his death) as *Journal of a Novel: The "East of Eden" Letters*, it offers rare insights into an extraordinary personality and the creative process. Reading it, you sense what it feels like to be a writer.

His diary during *East of Eden* shows he could poke fun at his work. On one April day he wrote, "I suppose that if I had any sense at all, I would not write today but I am going to anyway. It would be a great joke on the people in my book if I just left them high and dry, waiting for me. If they bully me and do what they choose I have them over a barrel. They can't move until I pick up a pencil. They are frozen, turned to ice standing one foot up and with the same smile they had yesterday when I stopped."

It was rarely, if ever, roses all the way. Steinbeck could slide into a tailspin. For three days, working on this novel, he said, "I went into a depression that was devastating. . . . It was very painful, hard on me, perhaps harder on Elaine. . . . I'm all weak and shaken." The gloom would descend on him every once in a while. Perhaps, he said, because "I have been drinking too much." He usually did this on a Saturday night, and on Sunday suffered "a fine, depressed hangover in which nothing seemed any good and I myself seemed the most no good of all."

Yet midway through the novel, he told himself, "You are having fun, aren't you? This is a time of great joy. It will never be so good again—never. A book finished, published, read—is always an anticlimax to me. The joy comes in the words going down and the rhythms crowding in the chest and pulsing to get out."

Steinbeck completed the rewriting stage in February 1952, and then decided he and Elaine needed a long vacation. *Collier's*, a popular magazine, gave him the opportunity. It commissioned him to travel abroad as a roving correspondent. They wanted personal pieces, his kind of human interest story about ordinary people that readers loved and learned from.

In March the Steinbecks left for North Africa aboard a freighter, stopping briefly in Casablanca and Algiers before crossing the Mediterranean to France, and then on to Spain. Here they stayed a while to watch several bullfights, as preparation for a piece John would write about a famous bullfighter named Litri.

While in Spain, John heard from his friend Elia Kazan that he had testified before the House Un-American Activities Committee. The Committee had been established in 1938 by conservatives in Congress to investigate supposed communist influence both in and out of government. It used the taint of communism to discredit progressive institutions and individuals. Accused of having been a communist himself, Kazan had named names, identifying friends he had worked with as communists. Such testimony became the main way for the accused to win pardon for their own "sins" and be restored to the good graces of conservatives.

Once publicly accused, such victims of the witch-hunt lost their jobs, their positions, their way of making a living. Some never worked again in their fields. Families were disrupted, professional lives crippled or destroyed, and some victims, unable to bear it, killed themselves.

Yet Steinbeck, writing to Pat Covici about the news of Kazan's testimony, said "He is a good and honest man. I hope the communists and the second-raters don't cut him to pieces now. But they can't hurt him very much."

The film director Jules Dassin, asked about what his friend Kazan and others had done, replied, "I think they simply placed career above honor. It's that simple. The need to work is very strong. And particularly in the arts—it's your oxygen. And their betrayal is a continuing pain because these are the guys I loved. And this still hurts."

Steinbeck seems to have forgotten how violently he had been attacked, accused of being a communist himself, when *The Grapes of Wrath* was published. Yet now he failed to support the writers and artists who were threatened. But when Lillian Hellman, the playwright, was also summoned by an investigating committee and refused to inform on others, Steinbeck privately defended what she did. "I understand both Hellman and Kazan," he wrote Covici. Was he saying that whatever a friend did was okay with him?

From Spain they went to Italy. Arriving in Venice, John heard from Kazan that he had just read *East of Eden* and wanted to make a movie of it. He reported that their joint effort, *Viva Zapata*, was now in the movie theaters and doing great business.

Viva Zapata, like the earlier novel *In Dubious Battle*, reflects Steinbeck's belief that power unrestrained can disrupt and destroy the struggle for justice. Earlier, on his trip to Russia, Steinbeck had seen one example of this, in the way the Commuist revolution had led not to the freedom it promised, but to the rigid control of almost every aspect of human society.

Around this time, Steinbeck in his journal notes the negative tone of much of contemporary fiction:

> The writers of today, even I, have a tendency to celebrate the destruction of the spirit and God knows it is destroyed often enough. It is the duty of the writer to lift up, to extend, to encourage. If the written word has contributed anything at all to our developing species and our half developed culture, it is this—great

writing has been a staff to lean on, a mother to consult, a wisdom to pick up stumbling folly, a strength in weakness and a courage to support weak cowardice. And how any despairing or negative approach can pretend to be literature, I do not know. It is true that we are weak and sick and ugly and quarrelsome but if that is all we ever were, we would, millenniums ago have disappeared from the face of the earth.

From Covici came word that big advance sales of *East of Eden* assured it of best-seller status. With that good news, the Steinbecks moved on to England, Scotland, and Ireland. They did not get back to New York until the end of August. John was now fifty, "a good age," he wrote his old friend Sheffield. "The hair recedes, the paunch grows a little, the face—rarely inspected, looks the same to us but not to others. The little inabilities grow so gradually that we don't even know it." As for his newest book, he told Sheffeld "it is the best work I have done but a lot of silly things are going to be said about it."

A month later the reviews of *East of Eden* began to appear. The *New York Times* said, though "clumsy in structure and defaced by excessive melodramatics and much cheap sensationalism," it was "on the whole a successful effort to grapple with a major theme." *Time* magazine, on the other hand, called it "a huge grab bag in which pointlessness and preposterous melodrama pop up as frequently as good storytelling and plausible conduct."

Perhaps the biographer Jay Parini's comparison of Steinbeck's two outstanding works may be helpful to readers:

> If *The Grapes of Wrath* may be read as a protest against the rough-edged individualism that dominated the first few decades of this century in America and led, perhaps necessarily, to the Great Depression, *East of Eden* may be read as a counterpoint, a protest against the maniacal conformity of the postwar years.

After all that running around in Europe, the Steinbecks' homelife in New York was quite tame. They led a quiet life, seeing a few friends, going out to dinner or the theater now and then. In his journal John wrote, "Oh! I am so happy—so very happy. I think I have never been so happy in my life. It seems absurd to feel so good about anything. Only the boys trouble me—nothing else. . . . And I love Elaine unbelievably, incredibly. I think this new life is entirely her doing. What joy."

This was 1952, a presidential election year, with General Dwight D. Eisenhower running on the Republican ticket and Adlai Stevenson, Governor of Illinois, the Democratic candidate. Steinbeck, a supporter of Roosevelt's New Deal reforms, volunteered to help Stevenson, whom he saw as a reformer, too. John wrote several speeches for the party's candidates. But Eisenhower won easily, placing the Republicans in control of the national government for the first time in twenty years.

Steinbeck and Stevenson did not meet until after the election, when a warm friendship developed. Once, writing Stevenson in a bleak mood, Steinbeck said, "Someone has to reinspect our system, and that soon. We can't expect to raise our children to be good and honorable men when the city, the state, the government, the corporations all offer the highest rewards for chicanery and dishonesty. . . . Maybe nothing can be done about it, but I am stupid enough and naively hopeful enough to want to try."

Early in 1953 the Steinbecks took a winter vacation in the Caribbean, a pattern they would follow for nine years. John always loved the theater, and hoped the characters of *Cannery Row* could be used in a musical. That never happened. Meanwhile he made use of the same characters in another novel, *Sweet Thursday.*

When Viking issued six of his short novels in one fat volume in 1953, he was jolted to see how much he had done and how much time had gone by. In that mood he wrote a friend that "a man has only a little to say and he says it over and over so it looks like a design. And the terrible thing is that I still don't know what it is I have to say, but I do know it isn't very complicated and surely it isn't new." It depressed him.

With *East of Eden* at the head of the best-seller list, he was again besieged by letters of all kinds and requests for interviews. Good news came, however, when Rodgers and Hammerstein, the top-rated creators of musicals, decided to convert *Sweet Thursday* into a musical to be called *Pipe Dream*.

At the close of winter, the Steinbecks planned a long vacation in Europe. They'd follow the spring season as it moved north from Spain and France into Scandinavia. Spain especially appealed to John. He loved the Cervantes novel *Don Quixote*, and thought perhaps he could create a book out of tracing that character's migration.

Soon after they reached France, John suffered a stroke, frighteningly worse than a very slight one he'd experienced some months earlier. Luckily it happened while in their hotel, where a doctor could provide immediate care.

Nevertheless they went on with the trip. The French loved his books—all of them. When a French literary weekly asked him to write short pieces for them, he said yes at once. He enjoyed this kind of work, and wrote something every week on his impressions of Paris. It was here that he learned his old friend Robert Capa had just been killed. He had stepped on a land mine in Korea while covering the war with his camera. Steinbeck was devastated. The two had become so close when working together, and this tragic event plunged him into fearful gloom. Was his end close, too?

While they were abroad, *Sweet Thursday* was published. It drew mixed reviews, like his other books. The nastiest said it was stuff salvaged from the wastebasket. Others praised it for being juicy and charming. Readers who knew his earlier fiction on the Monterey people saw how the character of Doc (Ed Ricketts) changed over the years in the way Steinbeck viewed him. In the end, the only thing that matters for Doc is love.

Writing to Elizabeth Otis from London, Steinbeck said that "style or technique may be a straitjacket which is the destroyer of a writer. It does seem true that when it becomes easy to write the writing is not likely to be any good. Facility can be the greatest danger in the world." Maybe he ought to dump his technique, he went on, and start all over?

In Rome, their next stop, he heard that Ernest Hemingway had won the Nobel Prize for literature. It pleased John greatly. He thought Hemingway should have been awarded it earlier. He was drawn to the beaches at Salerno again, and stood where he had witnessed the terrible slaughter of that invasion. It was like a "remembered nightmare," he said. From Naples they took a ship for home, reaching New York in time for the Christmas holidays.

Now they decided they wanted a permanent hangout for the summers. They found a cottage with two acres at Sag Harbor on Long Island. It sat right on the water's edge, and it had a boat dock, too. It needed lots of remodeling, which kept John busy all that spring. He'd loved the outdoors—boating, fishing, sailing—from childhood, and now he was assured of enjoying it in his own place, and with his beloved wife and children.

But what to do about writing? What next? A happy answer came when his agent made a deal with the *Saturday Review*, a much respected literary journal of liberal opinion. Beginning in 1955, Steinbeck would write editorial pieces from time to time, for several years. It was the kind of personal journalism he had loved doing ever since his series on California's migrant workers. His articles often dealt with hot topics such as the anti-communist witch-hunt, juvenile delin-quency, or issues the United Nations was contending with.

That fall, *Pipe Dream* opened on Broadway. Al-though the creation of great talents—Steinbeck, Rod-gers and Hammerstein—it failed. From rehearsals on, Steinbeck saw things wrong with it and tried hard to get specific changes made. But the two Broadway vet-erans ignored his criticism. The show lasted only six months on Broadway and never went on tour.

That ended John's desire to write for the stage. He turned back to fiction. This time, his mind was fixed on satirizing the reign of a king who happened also to be an intellectual—an astronomer. The book would be called *The Short Reign of Pippin IV.*

Intermixed with the fiction was more journalism. As the spring of 1956 came on, Steinbeck decided he'd like to report on the presidential nominating conven-tions of both major parties—the Republicans in San Francisco and the Democrats in Chicago. The Louis-ville *Courier Journal* signed him on and syndicated his dispatches to thirty-four other newspapers. He made no pretense of being a professional political reporter.

He promised only "printable copy." He'd write what he saw and heard and found amusing or illuminating.

He did have strong views of journalism, and in a letter to a staffer of the United States Information Bureau, he put it this way:

> What can I say about journalism? It has the greatest virtue and the greatest evil. It is the first thing the dictator controls. It is the mother of literature and the perpetrator of crap. In many cases it is the only history we have and yet it is the tool of the worst men. But over a long period of time and because it is the product of so many men, it is perhaps the purest thing we have. Honesty has a way of creeping in even when it was not intended.

That summer he worked on the *Pippin* manuscript, finding it lots of fun, though he was uncertain of its quality. His sons Thom and John, now eight and six, joined them at Sag Harbor. In August the Steinbecks flew to Chicago for the Democratic convention. John did much legwork at the convention, writing anecdotal pieces sparkling with his dry wit. Stevenson won the nomination, with John agreeing to write speeches to help the campaign. Then on to San Francisco, where the Republicans renominated Eisenhower and Nixon, as expected. There was little to write about there, so his pieces focused more on the city and its pleasures.

Afterwards the Steinbecks drove to Monterey, only to find it nothing like his old hangout—the canneries almost all gone, and the place transformed into a tourist town. Ed Ricketts gone, many others, too, dead or moved away. California would never again be at the heart of his work.

In the fall Steinbeck wrote some speeches for Stevenson and other party candidates, with little hope, for it was obvious that the Democrats hadn't a chance to win. Steinbeck was dejected by the party's failure to fight hard and openly on the issues as he saw them. He picked up polishing *Pippin* again. Neither his agent nor his publisher thought this book would go over big. But Steinbeck didn't seem to mind. In fact he was already thinking of trying another project set in bygone times, long, long ago. He wanted to retell the ancient legend of King Arthur and the knights of the Round Table.

It was the reliving of a childhood dream, when that story had fascinated him, as written in medieval English by Sir Thomas Malory in the fifteenth century. Steinbeck's aim was to translate it into modern English, "into simple, readable prose." Except for the Bible and perhaps Shakespeare, no book has had more effect on our morals than Malory's, he believed. It was a self-assigned scholarly task he delighted in pursuing. He collected all the books he could find dealing with that period of history and delved into the archival treasures of the superb Morgan Library in New York.

American sources weren't enough, however. He felt he must go abroad to see places where Malory himself had probably lived. Late in March 1957, the Steinbecks sailed for Italy.

TEN

WHILE IN ITALY, Steinbeck learned that the American playwright Arthur Miller, famous for his *Death of a Salesman*, had been indicted by the government for refusing to answer questions before the House Un-American Activities Committee. It was the same committee to whom the director Elia Kazan had given the names of friends and associates who had in the 1930s been communists. Steinbeck had defended Kazan then. Now, years later, he wrote an article for *Esquire* magazine in defense of Miller. In it he said.

> If I were in Arthur Miller's shoes, I do not
> know what I would do, but I could wish, for
> myself and for my children, that I would be

brave enough to fortify and defend my private morality as he has. I feel profoundly that our country is better served by individual courage and morals than by the safe and public patriotism which Dr. Johnson called "the last refuge of scoundrels."

And writing to his editor, Pat Covici, he added this:

I feel deeply that writers like me and actors and painters are in difficulty because of their own cowardice or perhaps failure to notice. When Artie [Arthur Miller] told me that not one writer had come to his defense, it gave me a lonely sorrow and a shame that I waited so long and it seemed to me also that if we had fought back from the beginning instead of running away, perhaps these things would not be happening now.

At the same time, in one of his pieces for the *Saturday Review*, he protested the State Department's policy of refusing visas to foreign writers, keeping them from entering the country. If the government thought their work was "dangerous" because of progressive or radical views, then the door was slammed on them. Ridiculing that policy, Steinbeck offered a list of some fifty great people from antiquity on down who regardless of their genius would have been kept out. No wonder, he learned, the PEN International Congress of Writers was never held in the United States. Too many of the most talented would be barred.

The Malory project would occupy Steinbeck for years. He went to Europe again and again to find connections that would bring the story alive for him. But nothing helped. He began to think his time for good writing was over. That feeling worsened when Alfred Kazin, a literary critic, asserted in the *New York Times* that Steinbeck had done little of value since *The Grapes of Wrath*.

Early in 1960 he turned away from Malory to begin work on a novel, *The Winter of Our Discontent*. The title is taken from the first lines of Shakespeare's play *King Richard III*:

Now is the winter of our discontent
Made glorious summer by this sun of York.

The setting of the novel is a fictional version of Sag Harbor, where the Steinbecks summered. The story is told by the central figure, Ethan Allen Hawley, an educated family man who lost his business to an unscrupulous man. Tempted, he follows that man's path to corruption in a marketplace where money is everything and honesty nothing. The reader feels that Steinbeck believes American culture has become thoroughly degraded.

"It isn't like anything I've ever done," Steinbeck said when he sent the draft around. "You may hate it." Neither his wife nor his agent nor his editor liked it. But others differed. The novelist Saul Bellow (who would win the Nobel Prize), when asked for an advance blurb, wrote, "John Steinbeck has returned to the high standards of *The Grapes of Wrath* and to the social themes that made his early work so impressive and so powerful."

Steinbeck's small strokes persisted, ominous signs of a rapidly deteriorating heart condition. Despite doctors' warnings, he decided to journey around the United States by himself that fall and to write about the experience. He surely knew that another heart attack could be the killer. But he was bound not to be treated like a cripple. Neither Elaine nor anyone else could talk him out of it.

In the title he gave the book—*Travels with Charley in Search of America*—he announces his aim. He didn't know his own country, he says. In writing about it in recent years he had been working only from memory. "I had not heard the speech of America, smelled the grass and trees and sewage, seen its hills and water, its color and quality of light. . . . So it was that I determined to look again, to try to rediscover this monster land."

To prepare, he had a truck manufacturer produce a three-quarter-ton truck, with a camper on top, and in it, a bed, stove, refrigerator, bath, lights, toilet, closet and storage space, windows. When it was delivered, he was delighted. He promptly named it *Rocinante*, after Don Quixote's horse.

He anticipated one big problem. He wanted to go as a nobody, yet his pictures had been so widely distributed by his publisher over many years, how could he go anywhere without being recognized and treated as a celebrity? That was the last thing he wanted. And what if nasty people decided to attack this lone old stranger? So he racked a shotgun, two rifles, and fishing rods on the truck. A stage setting he explained, for who would bother a hunter or fisherman?

Finally, to be gone so long without family or friends would be terribly lonely. "For this reason I took one companion on my journey—an old French gentleman poodle known as Charley. . . . A dog, particularly an exotic like Charley, is a bond between strangers."

He meant to do some writing while on the road. So he packed paper, pencils, notebooks, typewriter, dictionary, reference books. As the planned date of departure came close, he got the shakes. Was this trip crazy? The country suddenly seemed so huge, how could he ever cross it? Alone? At the age of fifty-eight?

In September he began with the New England states, and drove on to the Great Lakes region, the Dakotas, and the West Coast. There Elaine joined him for a while. Then he headed homeward, through Texas and Louisiana and up the East Coast.

Travels with Charley is a delightful book. You meet many interesting strangers and see many sights through the author's keen eyes, and all described with his ear for how people talk and his eye for significant detail.

One of the most memorable passages in the book occurs when Steinbeck drives into New Orleans. This is late in 1960, six years after the Supreme Court ruled that racial segregation of children in the public schools was unlawful.

While still in Texas, Steinbeck had seen pictures in the papers and on TV screens of white women gathered every day near the entrance of a New Orleans public school, screaming, cursing, threatening little African American children entering the school. A large crowd gathered every morning to watch the organized team of screamers, and cheer them on. In his book, Steinbeck said, "In a long and unprotected life I have seen and heard the vomitings of demonic humans before," but these screams filled him "with a shocked and sickened sorrow." He wondered, where were the many good people of New Orleans that he himself had known for years? The ones whose arms would ache to gather up the small, scared black kids?

"The crowd no doubt rushed home to see themselves on television, and what they saw went out all over the world, unchallenged by the other things I know are there."

During the long journey Steinbeck says that doubts were often in his thoughts—that is, doubts about the value of what he came away with. A reporter could interview all sorts of people in a community, then write about what he learned. But Steinbeck knew that another reporter might do the same thing and reach a totally different conclusion. Each person saw things his own way. No two outcomes might be alike. So what is the value of what I'm doing? he asked himself. Well, in the end it would be his own personal America set down on the page, and no one else's.

As Steinbeck was on his way home, John F. Kennedy was elected president. In January, Steinbeck was invited to attend the inauguration in Washington.

The Winter of Our Discontent was published that spring of 1961. The reviews were mixed. Steinbeck knew the novel had flaws, that he had limitations. But what difference does it make? he asked himself. Lord knows, he'd worked hard enough all these years—twenty-six books, and a lot of stories and essays. Maybe it was a relief to feel, here's a blank page. But I don't have to fill it. . . .

Steinbeck's sons—Thom, now seventeen, and

John, fifteen—were at this time students at a boarding school whose tuition was so high only the rich could afford it. Their mother Gwyn, who had not remarried, had sunk into such an alcoholic daze that her misbehavior had become too much for them. The boys packed their bags and moved in with their father and Elaine. He had them finish out the semester in a city school.

Steinbeck had long regretted his failure to connect intimately with his sons, and now he welcomed them warmly. This time he'd try harder to be a better father. He knew that, like other writers, he could be "mean, cantankerous, opinionated, quarrelsome, unreasonable, nervous, flighty . . ." He was sure his own father and mother often must have considered poisoning him.

As he completed *Travels with Charley*, Steinbeck decided the family needed a long vacation, a leisurely trip around the world. With them as the boys' tutor would go young Terrence McNally, who later became a successful playwright. So John, Elaine, the boys, and McNally sailed for England early in September. Steinbeck had mastered much of Britain's history while researching his Malory project and he enjoyed sharing it with the boys as they drove around the country. McNally's knowledge, too, was rich and deep and he had much to offer, though sometimes the boys rebelled at being pushed too hard. They'd thought this would be purely a vacation and not another form of schooling.

From Britain they crossed over into France, then on to Italy. In Milan the teenagers again fought against having to study, which made their father more and more agitated. Suddenly he fell unconscious—either a heart attack or a stroke. It was terribly scary, but he recovered quickly. It was thought it would be best if Steinbeck had a long rest while McNally took the boys to Florence, Venice, and the hill towns of Tuscany and Umbria. When the five reunited in Rome a month later for the Christmas holidays, Steinbeck was doing much better. Still, they realized they couldn't go around the world as they'd planned. Instead, they rented a villa on the island of Capri. Here Steinbeck did nothing at all, and "it seems to be working," he wrote Covici, "because I feel much better." He busied himself with reading the works of ancient historians of the Roman Empire.

On Capri he turned sixty. Deeply lined face, hair thinning and gray, dark circles under the eyes. He walked bent over and looked like an old man. He'd still go on working, but he knew it wouldn't be like anything he'd done before. They left Capri to tour southern Italy, Greece, and the Greek islands.

They were back in Sag Harbor to begin the summer season. *Travels with Charley* was published in July. It was received warmly by the *New York Times*. The *Atlantic* compared it to Thoreau's *Walden* as a book "to be quoted and measured by our own experience." There was higher praise for it than for anything he had done since *The Grapes of Wrath* thirty years before. And like that classic, it raced to the top of the best-seller lists.

Still, Steinbeck was not content. Again, he had the feeling that he would never write another book. He seemed fragile, though his health was a topic he tried to avoid.

Then, on October 25, 1962, as they were watching on TV developments in the Cuban missile crisis that threatened the peace, news flashed across their screen: John Steinbeck had just been awarded the Nobel Prize for Literature! They started dancing around the house and the phone began ringing and ringing as the press clamored for comments and friends and family called in their jubilation.

(Nobel prizes for outstanding achievement in several fields, without regard to nationality, were first awarded in 1901 by the will of the wealthy Swede Alfred Nobel.)

The next day Steinbeck was in Manhattan for a press conference Viking arranged. Stunned by this totally unexpected honor, Steinbeck barely managed to get through the barrage of press questions, while puffing on a cigar.

Steinbeck was the sixth American to win the Nobel for Literature, an honor accompanied, in 1962, by fifty thousand dollars. In his case, the award read: "For his realistic and imaginative writings, combining as they do sympathetic humour and keen social perception."

Several years before this, in a letter to Pat Covici, Steinbeck said he'd "be scared to death" to receive the Nobel Prize. "I don't care how coveted it is." He thought those who did win it "never do as good nor courageous a piece of work afterwards. . . . Maybe it

makes them respectable and a writer can't dare to be respectable."

The American writers who preceded him in receiving the Nobel award were Sinclair Lewis (1930), Eugene O'Neill (1936), Pearl S. Buck (1938), William Faulkner (1949), and Ernest Hemingway (1954). The *New York Times* ran an editorial lamenting that though Steinbeck had had a full career, he had "produced his major work more than two decades ago."

It was the same old story—his best work was way behind him. This could have been said of several of the other American prize-winners. Nevertheless, it hurt, and badly. And then other publications joined in, echoing the *Times*. But he received hundreds of letters from all around the world congratulating him.

The next concern was preparing his acceptance speech for the awards ceremony in Stockholm. He worried over what to say and how best to say it. Asking the opinion of others, he wrote at least twenty drafts of the speech, and recorded each draft to hear how it sounded. He and Elaine flew to Stockholm early in December for the ceremony. When the time came for

Steinbeck receiving the Nobel Prize for Literature in Stockholm, Sweden, December 10, 1962.

his acceptance, he thanked the Swedish Academy for finding his work "worthy of this highest honor," and said he doubted that he deserved it over other writers whom he respected. "Literature is as old as speech," he went on. "It grew out of human need for it, and it has not changed except to become more needed." The Swedish public felt a special warmth for Steinbeck, perhaps more than for most other American writers. There was little question that in Sweden he was the most popular choice for the prize. And this was probably true in other countries, too. His books had been translated into more than thirty languages.

When he returned home, he wrote his old friend Sheffield, "I want to write a small rude book and right away to get the taste of prizes out of my mouth. I'm about ready to start it. Maybe I can next week. It is for my own enjoyment."

And to another friend, Bo Beskow, he wrote, "Now is coming the time for recovery. As soon as Christmas is over and the boys back in school, I am going to withdraw completely into work and prove to myself that this not be an epitaph. It is a contract I have made with myself."

Once, asked by a university to comment on the nature of his work, Steinbeck replied: "My basic rationale might be that I like to write. I feel good when I am doing it—better than when I am not. I find joy in the texture and tone and rhythms of words and sentences, and when these happily combine in a thing that has texture and tone and emotion and design and architecture there comes a fine feeling—a satisfaction like that which follows good and shared love. If there have been difficulties and failures overcome, these may even add to the satisfaction."

Early in 1963, aging faster than he would admit, Steinbeck decided to move. Their townhouse on East Seventy-Second Street, with its steep stairs and lack of security, was now troublesome. He sold it and bought an apartment in a new building on the same street. Here he would remain till the end.

That spring, President Kennedy asked him to travel to the Soviet Union as part of a cultural exchange program, meant to ease tensions with that great power. Steinbeck replied he would go in the fall, but he hoped younger writers would join him, suggesting the playwright Edward Albee.

Shortly after moving to Sag Harbor for the summer, Steinbeck suffered a detached retina in one eye. Surgery was quickly done to correct the trouble, but it laid him up for weeks. His vision gradually returned. Feeling up to travel again, he visited Washington for a briefing by the State Department on what they hoped the Russian trip would accomplish. When he met with President Kennedy, Steinbeck made clear he didn't expect to be limited in what he might say.

In mid-October he and Elaine were in Moscow, together with Edward Albee. As someone not in the world spotlight, Albee would have a better chance to talk to dissenters in the communist country. And he did meet with more of them than Steinbeck was allowed to. Often such people just turned up unannounced, hoping not to be shadowed by a government agent. Steinbeck and Albee both talked to various groups of writers and went into schools, too. Sometimes, when student questions were hostile, they wondered if the secret police had planted them. Albee believed Steinbeck always said exactly what he thought. He didn't "make nice" to please anybody.

Through the Soviet Writers Union they met the

leading Russian writers, and lesser known ones, too. They all knew Steinbeck's work. Even his latest book, *The Winter of Our Discontent*, was already translated and on sale there—without any payment being made to Steinbeck. He didn't hesitate to complain loudly about that common practice of the Russians.

In Leningrad (renamed St. Petersburg in 1991), Steinbeck collapsed from exhaustion and was taken to a hospital. The doctors said he needed weeks of rest. But he refused to stay on, and a few days later was in communist Poland, meeting with writers and journalists and professors. While they were in Warsaw the news broke that President Kennedy had been assassinated in Dallas. It was shattering. The Poles tried their best to comfort them. The State Department told them to go to Vienna to rest awhile. From there they went on to Budapest, Prague, and West Germany. Everywhere it was the same—crowds welcoming a favorite author, people inviting them into their homes, lines at bookshops, fans begging for autographs.

Returning home, they went down to Washington, where Steinbeck reported on his mission, and then had dinner at the White House with the new president,

Lyndon B. Johnson. Mrs. Johnson and Elaine were old acquaintances, for they had attended the University of Texas together. After dinner the president insisted on walking them over to their nearby hotel. In the future, they'd stay at the White House when in Washington.

During the Christmas season, they were joined by Thom and John. But when the holidays ended, the young men went back to live with their mother, Gwyn. Steinbeck was terribly upset. Why couldn't they stay longer with him? Were he and Elaine to blame?

Terrence McNally, the boys' tutor during that long stay in Europe, had ample opportunity to observe the family interaction. He thought the tensions that commonly exist between a father and his sons in their adolescent years were part of the trouble. Then, too, Steinbeck's health had been deteriorating, and his drinking, his fear of worsening health, and his moodiness didn't help. He wanted to get close to his boys, but their mother's problems and her constant putdown of their father made things worse.

For some years, beginning at the age of five, each boy had been shipped off to summer camp, which they didn't like. And at nine, each had been sent to expensive boarding schools. Later, as an adult, John (Junior) recalled these schools as "dumping grounds" for the kids rich parents wanted to be rid of. He thought, too, that his father's "lifelong sense of inferiority" was appeased by sending his sons away to where the "best" people's kids went.

This may help to explain why, when their mother's behavior became too much for them, they fled to their father, and vice versa.

Steinbeck tried to get back to work. But not on a novel. Maybe pick up Malory again? He took out those notes for review. Then he switched to the idea of doing his autobiography, but who could be sure of what really happened way back when? How could he tell the difference between the facts and what his imaginative memory made up?

His summer at Sag Harbor got off to a fine start with the announcement that he would receive the Presidential Medal of Honor in September. This did not erase his low mood. He wrote to Pat Covici, "I consider the body of my work and I do not find it good. . . . If I have any more work in me, which I sometimes doubt, it will have to be of a kind to match my present age. I'm not the young writer of promise any more. I'm a worked-over claim. . . . More and more young people look at me in amazement because they thought I was dead."

Floundering for lack of the drive to initiate a project, he was rescued by his publisher. Viking had a collection of photographs illustrating many sides of American life. Would he write captions for them? He would indeed, but more than captions. He wrote little essays that tell readers just what he thought about many aspects of American life. Published in 1966 as *America and Americans*, the book added insights to *Travels with Charley*.

In October, Steinbeck lost one of his oldest and dearest friends, Pat Covici. His sudden death was "a dreadful shock. Only a writer can understand how a great editor is father, mother, teacher, personal devil and personal god. For thirty years Pat was my collaborator and my conscience. He demanded of me more than I had and thereby caused me to be more than I should have been without him."

It helped to have the sympathy of their new

friends—President and Mrs. Johnson. The Steinbecks were treated by the Johnsons like members of the family. The wives, Texans both, had much in common. And the men, both Westerners, shared a faith in President Roosevelt's New Deal goal: that government must open opportunity for a better life to all, regardless of creed or color. Steinbeck did what he could to help Johnson in such matters as drafting his acceptance speech at the 1964 Democratic nominating convention.

His skills as a writer and his immense prestige would be of great help to a political leader. He heartily approved it when Johnson pushed through Congress the Civil Rights Act outlawing segregation and the Equal Opportunity Act, which declared "war on poverty." Striving to create a Great Society, the president's plans culminated in still other laws affecting education, medical care, and voting rights. Though loyal to the president, Steinbeck had qualms about Johnson's readiness to make quick deals that sometimes compromised liberal goals.

A critical point in administration policy came in August 1964 when American troops began to assist

South Vietnam in its battle with the North Vietnamese and with communist guerrillas. Protests mounted in the streets and on college campuses against the military draft and deepening American involvement in the war. Steinbeck had two sons of military age. . . . What would happen to them?

ELEVEN

IN 1964, STEINBECK'S son John turned eighteen and was drafted. He had been living in California, where his mother had moved, and working as a disc jockey for a radio station. After basic training in Texas, he asked his father to use his influence with the president to have him sent promptly to Vietnam. Steinbeck replied, "I was horrified when you asked me to get you orders to go out, but I couldn't have failed you there. . . . But if I had had to request that you *not* be sent, I think I would have been far more unhappy." Thom, the older son, was already in the army, and in basic training in California. Steinbeck brought John to Washington, where he was photographed in uniform shaking hands with the President.

Years later, in an unfinished autobiography, son John said, "The war turned into a moral quicksand for

Dad as for many others. Though he himself knew better, he was somewhat blinded by the heady association with power." He added that "in the face of what he considered Communist aggression my father was becoming more and more conservative."

Because of his experience in radio, John was assigned to serve as a journalist in Vietnam for Armed Forces Radio and Television.

After his son had been in Vietnam for a few months, Steinbeck, ignoring his poor health, decided he had to go there, too, as a reporter for the Long Island paper, *Newsday*, for which he had been writing a regular column. In December 1966 he arrived in Southeast Asia with Elaine, and was met in Saigon by his son. Over the next six weeks he tried to see as many aspects of the war as possible, much as he had done in World War II.

One reason for going must have been his inability to get very far with any of the projects he'd hoped to do. Now he would see action, and that would give him plenty to write about. He spent most of the time in combat zones, then went back to the base to write his columns.

Steinbeck in Vietnam, 1966.

Elaine stayed in Saigon while he roved about, but there she, too, was in constant danger of a bomb exploding at any time in any place.

Steinbeck covered the fighting, risking his life everywhere he went. He flew in helicopters on assault missions and joined in ground attacks, too. None of the young soldiers had any idea who this old geezer was, climbing into a helicopter or walking through the jungle armed only with a cane. The pieces he sent to *Newsday* supported the war effort.

Back home, his syndicated columns angered many

who were against the war. By this time, people were opposing it in dozens of ways. They picketed and marched, they wore buttons and carried signs, they attended teach-ins and poetry read-ins, they signed anti-war advertisements and wrote letters to the editor. They staged mass protests in Washington in which hundreds of people were arrested. Three people burned themselves to death publicly in protest against the war. Draft-card burnings, too, were becoming common.

The mounting losses of sons, husbands, and fathers had made a great many Americans see Vietnam as an unhappy mistake, a departure from American tradition. Others tried to get Americans to see themselves as people abroad saw their country—an aggressive power determined to dictate to the rest of the world how they should live.

From Vietnam the Steinbecks traveled to other parts of Southeast Asia. Their expedition ended in Tokyo, where discs in John's spine fractured and he was confined to bed. When he was able to move, they returned home, settling in at Sag Harbor for the summer. Of course he couldn't stop thinking of all he'd seen in Vietnam, and admitted to friends he was sure the people running the war had no control over it. He believed that America could never win.

His back injury worsened, requiring surgery and a long hospital stay that fall.

Just before he entered the hospital, Steinbeck heard on the radio that his son John had been arrested for possession of marijuana. John, discharged from service, was now working in Washington for the Pentagon's Information Office. While still in the army, John had written a magazine article about widespread use of the drug by the soldiers in Vietnam. Of course the combination of a famous writer's son saying this, and the facts themselves, got immense publicity. On trial, John denied that the marijuana belonged to him, and the Washington jury, believing him, acquitted him.

Naturally Steinbeck was terribly upset by the whole business. It did little to bring father and son closer. Nor did Steinbeck become closer to his other son.

The operation for spinal fusion was difficult but successful. Recovery kept him in the hospital until early December. But when released, he found it hard to get back to work of any kind. He didn't feel he was making any real progress medically. Then mild strokes began to recur from time to time. He stayed in the city with Elaine, to be near the hospital in case the worst happened. By late fall he realized life was slipping away, and the end would come soon, despite all the medical care he was given. On December 20, 1968, at home in their Manhattan apartment, he fell into a coma and died of heart failure. He was sixty-six years old.

Two years before he died, Steinbeck wrote about how American literature had developed in his own lifetime. Now we can recognize his place in that gathering of great talents.

> Perhaps someone knows how the great change came which elevated American writing from either weak imitation or amusing unimportance to a position of authority in the whole world, to be studied and in turn imitated. It happened quickly. A Theodore Dreiser wrote the sound and smell of his people; a Sherwood Anderson perceived and set down secret agonies long before the headshrinkers discovered them. Suddenly the great ones stirred to life: Willa Cather, then Sinclair

Lewis, O'Neill, Wolfe, Hemingway, Faulkner. There were many others, of course—poets, short-story writers, essayists like Benchley and E. B. White. Their source was identical; they learned from our people and wrote like themselves, and they created a new thing and a grand thing in the world—an American literature about Americans. It was and is no more flattering than Isaiah was about the Jews, Thucydides about the Greeks, or Tacitus, Suetonius, and Juvenal about the Romans; but, like them, it has the sweet, strong smell of truth. And as had been so in other ages with other peoples, the Americans denounced their glory as vicious, libelous, and scandalous falsehood—and only when our literature was accepted abroad was it welcomed home again and its authors claimed as Americans.

NOTES

SOURCES FOR THE study of John Steinbeck's life and works are now immense in number. Scholars began researching him almost at the beginning of his literary career, and in the decades since his death such projects have multiplied. The Center for Steinbeck Studies at San Jose University in San Jose, California, houses a collection of over 40,000 items of Steinbeck memorabilia. The collection is open to scholars, students, and members of the community. Several Steinbeck-oriented periodicals exist; the leading one being *Steinbeck Studies* of California State University, San Jose.

Biographical research always presents problems, for no part of a subject's life is without confusion and complexity. John Steinbeck was born a little more than a hundred years ago. As a professional writer he left what seems to be ample evidence—his many works of fiction and nonfiction, and such documents as letters and diaries. As a very successful author there were numerous press interviews with him, and memoirs about him recorded by friends, family, and others.

Even when you have what seems to be useful evidence, it is often written by people with an ax to grind. They wish to make themselves or someone else look good—or bad. You need to be wary, for such material is always shaped by people with their own motives. No one can be purely objective.

Out of what the sources contain, the biographer seeks to create some arrangement or pattern in the life he has studied. Documentary evidence can be used in imaginative ways without departing from the truth. You try to give form to flux, to impose a design upon chronology. My task has been to find a way to re-create the world of my subject's life as he experienced it.

For the detailed chronicle of Steinbeck's life and a broad perspective on his literary achievement, Benson and Parini are invaluable. Steinbeck's personal struggle to create his work is most vividly presented in *Steinbeck: A Life in Letters* and in *Journal of a Novel: The East of Eden Letters*. His son John IV and that son's wife Nancy provide intimate views of Steinbeck in family life, while Fensch lets us overhear press interviews with him.

FOREWORD

"Writers are a sorry . . .": Steinbeck and Wallsten, *Steinbeck: A Life in Letters*, 642.

"Wish to God . . .": Steinbeck and Wallsten, *Steinbeck: A Life in Letters*, 484.

CHAPTER ONE

"the whole nasty bloody . . .": Benson, *John Steinbeck, Writer*, 612.

"singularly silent man . . .": Plimpton and Crowther, "John Steinbeck," 24.

"it was he . . .": Benson, *John Steinbeck, Writer*, 15.

"green gold": Steinbeck, *Travels with Charley*, xvii.

"an electric excitement": Steinbeck, *Travels with Charley*, 137.

"My father was . . .": Benson, *John Steinbeck, Writer*, 813.

"He was an almost . . .": Steinbeck, *America*, 125.

"When I was 16 or 17 . . .": Steinbeck and Wallsten, *Steinbeck: A Life in Letters*, 36.

"I remember them . . .": Benson, *John Steinbeck, Writer*, 23.

"When I was sixteen . . .": Steinbeck and Wallsten, *Steinbeck: A Life in Letters*, 654.

"so long as . . .": Benson, *John Steinbeck, Writer*, 44.

"The 'lean terse style' . . .": Benson, *John Steinbeck, Writer*, 59.

"one was perfectly . . .": Steinbeck and Wallsten, *Steinbeck: A Life in Letters*, 8.

CHAPTER TWO

"You will remember . . .": Steinbeck and Wallsten, *Steinbeck: A Life in Letters*, 18.

"as starved and happy a group . . .": Steinbeck and Wallsten, *Steinbeck: A Life in Letters*, 20.

CHAPTER THREE

"We pooled our . . .": Congdon, *The Thirties*, 24.

"capable of prodigies . . .": Steinbeck, *America*, 206.

"His mind had . . .": Steinbeck, *America*, 188.

"gets prettier all the time. . .": Steinbeck and Wallsten, *Steinbeck: A Life in Letters*, 37.

"Carol was important . . .": Benson, *John Steinbeck, Writer*, 181.

"tiny novels . . . very much.": Benson, *John Steinbeck, Writer*, 219.

"The haunting thought . . .": Benson, *John Steinbeck, Writer*, 214.

"slow torture": Benson, *John Steinbeck, Writer*, 272.

CHAPTER FOUR

"black blizzard": Fensch, *Steinbeck and Covici*, 126.

"light and I think . . .": Steinbeck and Wallsten, *Steinbeck: A Life in Letters*, 88.

"I felt them . . .": Steinbeck, *America*, 25.

"I didn't believe . . .": Steinbeck, *America*, 27.

"I don't know . . .": Benson, *John Steinbeck, Writer*, 304.

"If Steinbeck's organizers . . .": Benson, *John Steinbeck, Writer*, 304.

"my typing is . . .": Steinbeck and Wallsten, *Steinbeck: A Life in Letters*, 101.

"I am capable . . .": Steinbeck and Wallsten, *Steinbeck: A Life in Letters*, 103.

"a brutal book, more . . ." and "seem a little bit racy": Steinbeck and Wallsten, *Steinbeck: A Life in Letters*, 105.

"Neither side is willing . . .": Reef, *John Steinbeck*, 63.

"Curious that this second-rate . . .": Steinbeck, *Conversations*, 33.

"This is the first . . .": Steinbeck and Wallsten, *Steinbeck: A Life in Letters*, 119.

"of giant height . . .": McElrath, Crisler, and Shillinglaw, *Contemporary Reviews*, 39.

"The poor little fellow . . .": Benson, *John Steinbeck, Writer*, 327.

CHAPTER FIVE

"a litter of dirty . . .": Steinbeck, *Harvest Gypsies*, 26.

"There is more filth . . . legs of the children": Steinbeck, *America*, 79–80.

"A little man in . . .": Benson, *John Steinbeck, Writer*, 339.

"From the first . . .": Steinbeck, *Harvest Gypsies*, 39–40.

"The Associated Farmers, which . . .": Steinbeck, *America*, 84.

"for one of . . .": Benson, *John Steinbeck, Writer*, 347.

"The labor situation is . . .": Benson, *John Steinbeck, Writer*, 348.

"I must go . . .": Steinbeck and Wallsten, *Steinbeck: A Life in Letters*, 158.

"The suffering is too . . .": Steinbeck and Wallsten, *Steinbeck: A Life in Letters*, 161.

CHAPTER SIX

"the detailed description. . .": Steinbeck, *Working Days*, 29.

". . . in the eyes of the hungry . . .": Steinbeck, *Grapes of Wrath*.

"a genuinely great American . . .": McElrath, Crisler, and Shillinglaw, *John Steinbeck: The Contemporary Reviews*, 141.

"It will not . . .": Steinbeck and Wallsten, *Steinbeck: A Life in Letters*, 172.

"To Carol who . . .": Steinbeck and Wallsten, *Steinbeck: A Life in Letters*, 181.

"a lie, a black, infernal . . .": Benson, *John Steinbeck, Writer*, 418–19.

"as a careful reading makes . . .": Gibbs, "John Steinbeck," 195.

"I simply cannot . . .": Leonard, "Cozzens without Sex," 372.

"No novel of our . . .": McElrath, Crisler, and Shillinglaw, *John Steinbeck: The Contemporary Reviews*, 156.

"No punches were . . .": Benson, *John Steinbeck, Writer*, 411.

"I must face . . .": Steinbeck and Wallsten, *Steinbeck: A Life in Letters*, 352.

"the inconvenience and misery . . .": McWilliams, *California*, 160.

"shocking degree of . . .": Benson, *John Steinbeck, Writer*, 422.

CHAPTER SEVEN

"The world is . . . find a basic new picture.": Benson, *John Steinbeck, Writer*, 426.

"I can't tell . . .": Fensch, *Steinbeck and Covici*, 22.

"creative association between . . .": Benson, *John Steinbeck, Writer*, 429.

"the life of any . . .": Benson, *John Steinbeck, Writer*, 430.

"We knew that . . .": Steinbeck, *The Log*.

"darned fine book": Steinbeck, *Conversations with John Steinbeck*, 40.

"God knows I'm. . .": Steinbeck and Wallsten, *Steinbeck: A Life in Letters*, 232.

"it *could* happen . . .": Benson, *John Steinbeck, Writer*, 488.

"a curious, crazy and yet . . .": Steinbeck, *Once There Was a War*, 10.

"He might have . . .": Benson, *John Steinbeck, Writer*, 531.

"Perhaps all experience . . .": Steinbeck, *Once There Was a War*, 124.

"after the war . . .": Benson, *John Steinbeck, Writer*, 495.

"we'll get along . . .": Steinbeck and Wallsten, *Steinbeck: A Life in Letters*, 240.

"'An exciting time' . . .": Steinbeck and Wallsten, *Steinbeck: A Life in Letters*, 271.

CHAPTER EIGHT

"write something funny . . .": Steinbeck, *America*, 160.

"a frightful pounding": Steinbeck and Wallsten, *Steinbeck: A Life in Letters*, 279.

"Early morning is . . .": Steinbeck, *Cannery Row*, 77.

"a lot of the little boy . . .": Plimpton and Crowther, "John Steinbeck," 8.

"One of the most . . .": Steinbeck, *America*, 123.

"amazing . . . new or old.": Benson, *John Steinbeck, Writer*, 674.

"it's the whole nasty . . .": Benson, *John Steinbeck, Writer*, 612.

"No one who knew him . . .": Steinbeck, *America*, 182.

CHAPTER NINE

"in trouble in some way . . .": Steinbeck, *Journal of a Novel*, 12.

"in some deep emotional trouble . . .": Steinbeck, *Journal of a Novel*, 25.

"a huge grab . . .": McElrath, Crisler, and Shillinglaw, *John Steinbeck: The Contemporary Reviews*, 395.

"I suppose that . . .": Steinbeck, *Journal of a Novel*, 61.

"I went into a depression . . .": Steinbeck, *Journal of a Novel*, 45.

"I have been drinking . . .": Steinbeck, *Journal of a Novel*, 3.

"a fine, depressed hangover . . .": Steinbeck, *Journal of a Novel*, 13.

"You are having . . .": Steinbeck, *Journal of a Novel*, 132.

"He is a good . . .": Steinbeck and Wallsten, *Steinbeck: A Life in Letters*, 443.

"I think they . . .": McGilligan and Buhle, *Tender Comrades*, 203.

"I understand both . . .": Parini, *John Steinbeck*, 357.

"The writers of today . . .": Fensch, *Steinbeck and Covici*, 189.

"a good age" and "it is the best . . .": Benson, *John Steinbeck, Writer*, 730.

"clumsy in structure . . .": McElrath, Crisler, and Shillinglaw, *John Steinbeck: The Contemporary Reviews*, 383.

"a huge grab . . .": McElrath, Crisler, and Shillinglaw, *John Steinbeck: The Contemporary Reviews*, 395.

"If *The Grapes of Wrath* may be . . .": Parini, *John Steinbeck*, 365.

"Oh! I am so happy . . .": Steinbeck, *Journal of a Novel*, 13.

"Someone has to . . .": Steinbeck and Wallsten, *Steinbeck: A Life in Letters*, 653.

"a man has only . . .": Steinbeck and Wallsten, *Steinbeck: A Life in Letters*, 474–75.

"style or technique . . .": Benson, *John Steinbeck, Writer*, 766.

"remembered nightmare": Steinbeck and Wallsten, *Steinbeck: A Life in Letters*, 501.

"printable copy" and "What can I . . .": Steinbeck and Wallsten, *Steinbeck: A Life in Letters*, 526.

"into simple, readable . . .": Benson, *John Steinbeck, Writer*, 804.

CHAPTER TEN

"If I were . . ." and "I feel deeply . . .": Benson, *John Steinbeck, Writer*, 813.

"It isn't like . . .": Parini, *John Steinbeck*, 431.

"You may hate . . .": Benson, *John Steinbeck, Writer*, 880.

"John Steinbeck has . . .": McElrath, Crisler, and Shillinglaw, *John Steinbeck: The Contemporary Reviews*, 460.

"I had not . . .": Steinbeck, *Travels with Charley*, 5.

"For this reason . . .": Steinbeck, *Travels with Charley*, 7–8.

"In a long and unprotected . . .": Steinbeck, *Travels with Charley*, 195.

"The crowd no doubt . . .": Steinbeck, *Travels with Charley*, 196.

"mean, cantankerous, opinionated . . .": Steinbeck and Wallsten, *Steinbeck: A Life in Letters*, 550.

"it seems to . . .": Steinbeck and Wallsten, *Steinbeck: A Life in Letters*, 734–35.

"to be quoted . . .": Benson, *John Steinbeck, Writer*, 913.

"For his realistic . . .": Wright and Wright, *Universal Almanac*, 586.

"be scared to . . ." "I don't care . . ." and "never do as . . .": Steinbeck and Wallsten, *Steinbeck: A Life in Letters*, 527.

"produced his major . . .": Benson, *John Steinbeck, Writer*, 915.

"worthy of this . . .": Benson, *John Steinbeck, Writer*, 919.

"Literature is as . . .": Benson, *John Steinbeck, Writer*, 920.

"I want to . . .": Benson, *John Steinbeck, Writer*, 921.

"Now is coming . . .": Steinbeck and Wallsten, *Steinbeck: A Life in Letters*, 759.

"My basic rationale . . .": Steinbeck, *America*, 161.

"dumping grounds" and "lifelong sense of . . .": Steinbeck and Steinbeck, *Other Side of Eden*, 71

"I consider the body . . .": Benson, *John Steinbeck, Writer*, 960.

"a dreadful shock. Only . . .": Benson, *John Steinbeck, Writer*, 961.

CHAPTER ELEVEN

"I was horrified . . .": Benson, *John Steinbeck, Writer*, 988.

"The war turned into . . ." and "in the face of . . .": Steinbeck and Steinbeck, *Other Side of Eden*, 99.

"Perhaps someone knows . . .": Steinbeck, *America*, 388.

BOOKS BY
JOHN STEINBECK

Cup of Gold: A Life of Sir Henry Morgan, Buccaneer, with Occasional Reference to History. New York: Robert M. McBride & Company, 1929.

The Pastures of Heaven. New York: Brewer, Warren and Putnam, 1932.

To a God Unknown. New York: Robert O. Ballou, 1933.

Tortilla Flat. New York: Covici-Friede, 1935.

In Dubious Battle. New York: Covici-Friede, 1936.

Of Mice and Men. Separate editions of play and novel. New York: Covici-Friede. 1937.

The Red Pony. New York: Covici-Friede, 1937.

Their Blood Is Strong. San Francisco: Simon J. Lubin Society, 1938.

The Long Valley. New York: The Viking Press, 1938.

The Grapes of Wrath. New York: The Viking Press, 1939.

Sea of Cortez: A Leisurely Journal of Travel and Research with a Scientific Appendix. With Edward F. Ricketts. New York: The Viking Press, 1941.

The Forgotten Village. New York: The Viking Press, 1941.

Bombs Away: The Story of a Bomber Team. New York: The Viking Press, 1942.

The Moon Is Down. New York: The Viking Press, 1942.

The Moon Is Down: A Play in Two Parts. New York: Dramatists' Play Service, 1942.

Cannery Row. New York: The Viking Press, 1945.

The Wayward Bus. New York: The Viking Press, 1947.

The Pearl. New York: The Viking Press, 1947.

A Russian Journal. New York: The Viking Press, 1948.

Burning Bright. New York: The Viking Press, 1950.

The Log from the "Sea of Cortez." New York: The Viking Press, 1951.

East of Eden. New York: The Viking Press, 1952.

Sweet Thursday. New York: The Viking Press, 1954.

The Short Reign of Pippin IV: A Fabrication. New York: The Viking Press, 1957.

Once There Was a War. New York: The Viking Press, 1958.

The Winter of Our Discontent. New York: The Viking Press, 1961.

Travels with Charley in Search of America. New York: The Viking Press, 1962.

America and Americans. New York: The Viking Press, 1966.

Journal of a Novel: The "East of Eden" Letters. New York: The Viking Press, 1969.

Viva Zapata! Screenplay of 1952 film. New York: The Viking Press, 1974.

Steinbeck: A Life in Letters. Edited by Elaine Steinbeck and Robert Wallsten. New York: The Viking Press, 1975.

The Acts of King Arthur and His Noble Knights: From the Winchester Manuscript and Other Sources. Edited by Chase Horton. New York: Farrar, Straus & Giroux, 1976.

Working Days: The Journal of "The Grapes of Wrath." Edited by Robert DeMott. New York: The Viking Press, 1989.

The Grapes of Wrath and Other Writings, 1936–1941. New York: The Library Of America, 1996.

BIBLIOGRAPHY

Benson, Jackson J. *John Steinbeck, Writer: A Biography*. New York: Penguin, 1990.

Congdon, Don, editor. *The Thirties: A Time to Remember*. New York: Simon & Schuster, 1962.

Fensch, Thomas. *Steinbeck and Covici: The Story of a Friendship*. New Century Books, 2002.

Gibbs, Lincoln R. "John Steinbeck, Moralist." *The Antioch Review*. Vol. 17, 1956.

Leonard, Frank G. "Cozzens without Sex, Steinbeck without Sin." *The Antioch Review*. Vol. 2, 1942.

Lisca, Peter. *The Wide World of John Steinbeck*. New Brunswick, N.J.: Rutgers University Press, 1958.

McElrath, Joseph R., Jesse S. Crisler, and Susan Shillinglaw. *John Steinbeck: The Contemporary Reviews*. Cambridge University Press, 1996.

McGilligan, Patrick and Paul Buhle. *Tender Comrades*. New York: St. Martin's Press, 1997.

McWilliams, Carey, and Lewis H. Lapham, contributor. *California: The Great Exception*. Berkeley: University of California Press, 1999.

Meltzer, Milton. *Dorothea Lange: A Photographer's Life*. New York: Farrar, Straus & Giroux, 1978. Reprint, Syracuse University Press, 2000.

Meltzer, Milton. *Walt Whitman: A Biography*. Brookfield, Conn.: Twenty-First Century Books, 2002.

Mitchell, Don. *The Lie of the Land: Migrant Workers and the California Landscape*. Minneapolis: University of Minnesota Press, 1996.

Parini, Jay. *John Steinbeck: A Biography*. New York: Henry Holt & Co., 1995.

Plimpton, George, and Frank Crowther. "John Steinbeck, The Art of Fiction No. 45." *The Paris Review*, Vol. 48, Fall 1969.

Reef, Catherine. *John Steinbeck*. New York: Clarion Books, 1996.

Sheffield, Carlton A. *John Steinbeck: The Good Companion*. Portola Valley, Calif.: American Lives Endowment, 1983.

St. Pierre, Brian. *John Steinbeck: The California Years*. San Francisco: Chronicle, 1983.

Stein, Walter J. *California and the Dust Bowl Migration*. Westport, Conn.: Greenwood Press, 1973.

Steinbeck, Elaine, and Robert Wallsten, editors. *Steinbeck: A Life in Letters*. New York: Penguin, 1989.

Steinbeck, John. *America and Americans and Selected Nonfiction.* New York: Penguin, 2003.

Steinbeck, John. *Cannery Row (Centennial Edition).* New York: Penguin, 2002.

Steinbeck, John. *Conversations with John Steinbeck.* Edited by Thomas Fensch. Jackson: University Press of Mississippi, 1988.

Steinbeck, John. *The Grapes of Wrath.* New York: Penguin, 2006.

Steinbeck, John. *The Harvest Gypsies: On the Road to the Grapes of Wrath.* Berkeley, Calif.: Heyday Books, 1988.

Steinbeck, John. *Journal of a Novel: The East of Eden Letters.* New York: Penguin, 1990.

Steinbeck, John. *Once There Was a War.* London: Corgi, 1961.

Steinbeck, John. *The Log from the Sea of Cortez.* New York: Penguin, 1995.

Steinbeck, John. *Travels with Charley.* New York: Penguin, 1997.

Steinbeck, John, IV, and Nancy Steinbeck. *The Other Side of Eden: Life with John Steinbeck.* Amherst, N.Y.: Prometheus Books, 2001.

Tedlock, E. W., Jr., and C. W. Wicker, eds. *Steinbeck and His Critics.* Albuquerque: University of New Mexico Press, 1957.

Wright, John W. II, and John W. Wright. *The Universal Almanac 1992.* Kansas City, Mo.: Andrews McMeel, 1991.

INDEX

Abramson, Ben, 80, 101

Air Force, U.S., 136

Air Force Aid Society Trust Fund, 137

Albee, Edward, 199–200

Allee, W. C., 62

America and Americans (Steinbeck), 204

American Academy of Arts and Letters, 116, 162

American Communist Party, 76–77

Anderson, Sherwood, 35, 212

Associated Farmers, 95, 97, 116, 126

Atlantic, 194

Bailey, Margery, 35

"Battle Hymn of the Republic," 113–14, 117

Bellow, Saul, 187

Benchley, Margery, 151–52

Benchley, Nathaniel, 151–53, 155–56, 159, 213

Benson, Jackson, 65, 83

Beskow, Bo, 198

Between Pacific Tides (Ricketts), 119–20

"bindlestiffs," 31, 32

Blaine, Mahlon, 42, 43, 44–45

Bombs Away: The Story of a Bomber Team (Steinbeck), 136–37

Book-of-the-Month Club, 98

Boren, Lyle, 118

Brigham, Mrs. Alice, 46, 48, 49

Buck, Pearl S., 197

Burns, Robert, 86

Cagney, James, 101

California
    landscape of, 20
    migrant workers in, *see* migrant workers
    migration to, 72–73, 80
    statehood, 20

California State Relief Administration, 83

Cannery and Agricultural Workers Union, 76–77

Cannery Row (film), 159

Cannery Row (Steinbeck), 63, 132, 14 , 146–48, 176

Capa, Robert, 156, 157, 158–59, 177–

Cather, Willa, 212

Chambers, Pat, 81, 82

Chaplin, Charlie, 116

Civil Rights Act of 1964, 205

Cold War, 157–58

Collier's, 169–70

Collins, Tom, 93–94, 96, 99, 101, 102, 104, 117, 122
Commonwealth Club of California, 85
Condon, Eddie, 153
Congress of Industrial Organizations (CIO), 108
Covici, Pascal (Pat), 80, 84, 88, 99, 113, 130, 160, 167, 171, 185, 193, 203
    death of, 204
Covici-Friede, 80, 84–85, 113
Crane, Stephen, 43
Cup of Gold (Steinbeck), 41, 42, 44, 48, 49–50
    publication of, 54, 55
Cupp, Miss, 25

Dassin, Jules, 171
Day, A. Grove, 54
de Kruif, Paul, 124
Don Quixote (Cervantes), 177
Dostoyevsky, Fyodor, 25
Drama Critics Circle, 101
Dreiser, Theodore, 43, 212
Dust Bowl, 13, 70, 72, 80, 106, 110

East of Eden (film), 172
East of Eden (Steinbeck), 159, 164, 166–69, 172
    reviews of, 174
    success of, 173, 176–77
Eisenhower, Dwight D., 175, 182
Eliot, George, 25
Equal Opportunity Act, 205
squire, 184

Factories in the Fields (McWilliams), 124
Farm Security Administration, 101, 102
Faulkner, William, 55, 197, 213
Federal Bureau of Investigation (FBI), 116
Fernandez, Emilio, 148
Fight for Life, The, 120–21
Fitzgerald, F. Scott, 30
Flaubert, Gustave, 25
Ford, John, 122
Foreign Information Service, U.S., 134
Forgotten Village, The, 130–31
Frost, Robert, 30

Germany, World War II and, 124, 131, 134, 135, 149, 156
Gold Rush of 1849, 72–73
Grapes of Wrath, The (film), 106, 121, 122
    ending of, 111, 115–16
Grapes of Wrath, The (Steinbeck), 11, 13, 17, 174
    dedication of, 117
    publication of, 13, 114–15
    reaction to, 117–19, 124–26
    research for, 101–2, 104–6
    reviews of, 117–18
    success of, 119, 121, 124
    title of, 113–14
    writing of, 109–12, 114
Great Depression, 57–58, 64, 68–69, 79–80
    farming and farmworkers and, 70–76
Gregory, Susan, 74

Hamilton, Joe (uncle), 43
Hamilton, Samuel (paternal grandfather), 17
Hamilton family, 22, 167
Hardy, Thomas, 25
Hellman, Lillian, 171
Hemingway, Ernest, 43, 55, 178–79, 197, 213
Henning, Carol, see Steinbeck, Carol Henning (first wife)
Henning family, 61
Hitchcock, Alfred, 138
Hitler, Adolf, 69
House Un-American Activities Committee, 170, 171, 184–85
Howe, Julia Ward, 113–14
Hyman, Stanley Edgar, 118

immigration, 16
In Dubious Battle (Steinbeck), 81–83, 84, 88
In Our Time (Hemingway), 55
Italy, World War II and, 135
Ivanhoe (Scott), 23

Japan, World War II and, 124, 135, 149
Johnson, Lady Bird, 202, 204–5
Johnson, Lyndon B., 201–2, 204–6
Great Society, 205
Johnson, Nunnally, 122
"John Steinbeck Committee to Aid Agricultural Organization," 108
Journal of a Novel: The "East of Eden" Letters, 167–69

Katrina, 41–42

Kaufman, George S., 100
Kazan, Elia, 162, 170–71, 172, 184
Kazin, Alfred, 186
Kennedy, John F., 191, 199, 200
assassination of, 201
King Arthur and the knights of the Round Table, 23, 182–83
see also Malory, Sir Thomas
King Haakon Liberty Cross, 154
King Richard III, 186
Kirkland, Jack, 103
Kline, Herbert, 130
Korean War, 177–78
Kronenberg, Louis, 119

labor, 16, 32
migrant workers, see migrant workers
New Deal and, 79–80
LaFollette, Robert M., 126
Lange, Dorothy, 107
Last of the Mohicans, The (Cooper), 23
Lewis, Sinclair, 35, 197, 212–13
Life, 106
Lifeboat, 137–38, 142
London, Jack, 31, 35
Long Valley, The (Steinbeck), 68, 113, 115
Lorentz, Pare, 106–7, 120, 124
Los Gatos, California, Steinbeck home in, 86, 87, 112, 133
Louisville Courier Journal, 180–81
Lubin Society, Simon J., 107–8

McBride, Robert, 54
McIntosh, Mavis, 66, 84
McKiddy, Cicil, 80, 81

McNally, Terrence, 192, 193, 202
McWilliams, Carey, 124
Madison Square Garden, 42
Malory, Sir Thomas, 23
    John's project on, 183, 186, 192–93,
        203
Medal for Benny, A, 137
Mexico, migrant workers from, *see*
    migrant workers
migrant workers, 13, 16, 75–76, 125
    Grapes of Wrath, see Grapes of Wrath,
        The (Steinbeck)
    San Francisco News articles on, 88–98
    Spreckels and, 31–32, 33–34
    strikes by, 75–76, 80–83, 95
    of Tulare County, 104–7
    unions, 76–77, 108
Milestone, Lewis, 116, 121, 133, 159
Miller, Arthur, 184–85
Miller, Ted, 50, 54, 61, 66
Mirrielees, Edith, 35–36
Moffet, Pickles, 24
Monterey, California, 182
    John's homes in, 132, 133, 144, 150
Monterey Trader, 107
Moon Is Down, The (film), 135
Moon Is Down, The (play), 135
Moon Is Down, The (Steinbeck), 134–35,
    154
Morgan, Sir Henry, 44
Morgan Library, New York, 183
Mors, George, 31
Mussolini, Benito, 69

Newsday, 208, 209
New York American, 43, 44

New York City, New York
    John moves to, 133–34
    John's homes in, 138, 149, 150, 151,
        166, 199
New York Herald Tribune, 138, 139, 156
New York Times, 186, 194, 197
Nixon, Richard M., 182
Nobel Prize for Literature, 11, 178–79,
    187, 194–98
North American Review, 78

Of Mice and Men (film), 101, 116, 121–22
Of Mice and Men (play), 100–101, 103
Of Mice and Men (Steinbeck)
    plot of, 87
    publication of, 88
    reception for, 98–99
    title of, 86
    writing of, 86–87
"Okies," 73
Once There Was a War, 139, 140–41
O'Neill, Eugene, 197, 213
Otis, Elizabeth, 66, 87–88, 104, 106, 115,
    116, 122, 123, 128, 132, 178

Pacific Biological Laboratories, 62
Pacific Grove, California, Steinbeck
    family cottage in, 21–22, 53, 58, 61–62,
    67
Paramount, 86
Parini, Jay, 174
Pastures of Heaven, The (Steinbeck), 65,
    66
Pearl, The (film), 142, 148, 149, 151, 153
Pearl, The (Steinbeck), 142–43, 148, 149
Pearl Harbor, attack on, 135

PEN International Congress of Writers, 186

Philippines, migrant workers from the, *see* migrant workers

Pipe Dream, 177, 180

Plow That Broke the Plains, The (Lorentz), 106–7

presidential elections
of 1952, 175–76
of 1956, 180–82

Presidential Medal of Honor, 203

Pulitzer Prize, 117

Red Pony, The (film), 133, 159

Red Pony, The (Steinbeck), 68, 78

Resettlement Administration, migrant farmworkers camps and, 89–96, 101

Ricketts, Edward, 87, 119–20, 127–28, 129
death of, 160–61, 182
described, 62–63
friendship with John, 62–63, 64, 66–67, 99, 123, 144, 149, 160
as model for John's characters, 62, 144, 178

Rodgers and Hammerstein, 177, 180

Roosevelt, Eleanor, 79, 125

Roosevelt, Franklin D., 79, 120, 131, 149
New Deal, 69, 79–80, 99, 205

Roosevelt, Theodore, 16

Sag Harbor, John's cottage in, 179, 181, 187, 203, 210

Salinas, California, 15, 16, 17–21, 65, 98
lettuce crops, 20, 21

Salinas High School, 24–25

San Francisco Chronicle, 52, 85

San Francisco News, 88
John's articles on California migrant farmworkers for, 88–98

Saturday Review, 179–80, 185–86

Scott, Waverly, 166

Sea of Cortez, The (Steinbeck), 130, 132

Senate Committee on Education and Labor, 126

Shebley, Lloyd, 48, 50

Sheffield, Carlton, 35, 38, 46, 56
correspondence with, 49, 127, 173

Short Reign of Pippin IV, 180, 181, 182

short stories of John Steinbeck, 32–33, 44–45, 48, 61, 65, 66
collections of, 68, 78, 113, 115

Sinclair, Upton, 35

socialism, 32, 52–53, 67

Social Security Act of 1935, 80

Solow, Eugene, 121

Soviet Union, 53, 99, 100, 156, 157–58, 159, 172, 199–201

Spreckels sugar plant, 20, 31–32, 33, 38

Stalin, Josef, 100

Stanford Spectator, 37

Stanford University, 30–31, 32–33, 34–39, 54
Hopkins Marine Station, 37

"Starvation Under the Orange Trees," 107

State Department, U.S., 185–86, 200, 201

Steinbeck, Beth (sister), 17, 30, 42, 68, 144, 148

Steinbeck, Carol Henning (first wife), 113, 117
  courtship, 50–51, 52, 53
  end of marriage, 131–33, 136
  jobs of, 66–67, 83
  marriage, 55–56, 60
  married life, 58–60, 64–66, 66–68, 85, 86, 87, 99–100, 101, 103–4, 109, 122–24, 129
  separation, 122–23
  social conscience of, 60, 77
  typing of John's manuscripts, 83–84, 104, 114
Steinbeck, Elaine Anderson Scott (third wife), 163–64, 166
  the Johnsons and, 202, 205
  marriage of, 164
  married life, 169, 170, 173, 174–75, 176, 177, 183, 188, 189, 192–93, 197, 200, 208–10, 212
  in Vietnam, 208, 209
Steinbeck, Esther (sister), 17, 30, 68, 144
Steinbeck, Gwyndolyn Conger (second wife), 131–32, 192
  divorce, 161–62
  health of, 159, 160
  marriage of, 133–34, 136
  married life, 138, 141–42, 148–61
  as mother, 143, 151, 153, 157, 166, 202
Steinbeck, John
  alcohol and, 31, 42, 51, 99, 145
  ancestry, 17
  appearance of, 25, 85
  birth of, 15
  childhood of, 17–29
  death of, 212
  depression, 31, 141, 145, 162, 169
  early interest in writing, 25, 26, 28–29, 32–33, 35–37, 38–39
  ecology and the environment and, 37–38, 61, 62, 127–30
  education of, 11, 22–26, 29–31, 32–33, 34–39
  as father, 143–44, 153, 158, 159, 162–63, 164–66, 175, 181, 192, 202–3, 211
  financial security, 84–85, 86, 99, 137
  first professional publication, 48
  foreign publication of works of, 100, 135, 154, 157, 177, 198, 201
  generosity of, 98, 103, 106, 117, 137
  the Great Depression and, 57–59, 64–66
  health of, 26, 58, 115, 121, 132, 160, 177, 187–88, 193, 201, 208, 210, 211–12
  imagination of, 22–23, 32, 152
  as journalist, *see specific publications*
  marine biology, interest in, 37–38, 48, 62, 120, 127–30
  marriages, *see* Steinbeck, Carol Henning (first wife); Steinbeck, Elaine Anderson Scott (third wife); Steinbeck, Gwyndolyn Conger (second wife)
  music, love of, 23, 111, 153
  negative attacks on, 116–17, 124–25, 138, 171

New York City, move to, 133–34

Nobel Prize for Literature, 11, 194–98

novels, *see individual titles*

photographs of, 18, 24, 40, 60, 165, 196

physical labor and assorted jobs, 26–28, 33–34, 38, 42–43, 44, 45, 46, 50, 51–52, 53

publicity and, 85, 99, 118–19, 176–77

reading his work to others, 29, 36–37

short stories, *see* short stories of John Steinbeck

on writers and writing, 11–12, 48–50, 172–73

writing process, 38–39, 83–84, 111, 114, 137, 167–69

Steinbeck, John, Jr. (son), 202–3

birth of, 153

childhood of, 154, 156, 157, 159, 162–63, 164–65, 175, 181, 191–94

marijuana charge, 211

military service, 207

Steinbeck, John Ernst (father), 17–19, 29–30, 31, 33, 42, 56

death of, 74

failing health of, 68, 74

influence on John Steinbeck, 22

support for John Steinbeck's writing, 19, 46, 53, 67

temperament of, 22, 34

Steinbeck, Mary (sister), 17, 18, 23, 68, 144

Steinbeck, Thom (son), 27, 28

birth of, 143–44

childhood of, 148, 149, 150, 151, 153, 154, 156, 157, 159, 162–63, 164–66, 175, 181, 191–94, 202–3

Vietnam War and, 207–8

Steinbeck, Olive Hamilton (mother), 17, 26, 34, 48–49, 56, 65

aspirations for John Steinbeck, 19

death of, 74

education of John Steinbeck and, 22–23, 29–30, 33

failing health, 67–68, 74

social injustice and, 22, 60

Stevenson, Adlai, 175–76, 182

stock market crash of 1929, 57

Story Writer, The (Mirrielees), 36

Stowe, Harriet Beecher, 119

Street, Webster, 35, 143

Sun Also Rises, The (Hemingway), 55

Sweet Thursday (Steinbeck), 63, 176, 178

Theatre Guild, 164

Their Blood Is Strong, 107

Thomsen, Eric, 90

Thoreau, Henry David, 47, 194

To a God Unknown (Steinbeck), 60–61, 6

"To a Mouse," 86

Tortilla Flat (play), 103

Tortilla Flat (Steinbeck), 32, 63, 68, 74, 84–85

publication of, 80, 84–85

reviews of, 85

Travels with Charley in Search of America (Steinbeck), 187–91, 192, 194

Treasure Island (Stevenson), 23

Twentieth Century-Fox, 122, 138

Uncle Tom's Cabin (Stowe), 119
unions, 76–77, 108
    see also migrant workers
United Cannery, Agricultural, Packing,
    and Allied Workers of America, 108

Vietnam for Armed Forces Radio and
    Television, 208
Vietnam War, 206–11
Viking Press, 84, 113, 114–15, 117, 176,
    195, 204
Viva Zapata (film), 162, 164, 172

Wagner, Jack, 137
Wagner, Max, 121, 139
Walden: or, Life in the Woods (Thoreau),
    47, 194
War Department, U.S., 138
Wayward Bus, The (Steinbeck), 150, 151,
    153–54, 155
Whitaker, Francis, 67, 77
White, E. B., 213
Wilhelmson, Carl, 35, 55, 66
Winter of Our Discontent, The
    (Steinbeck), 186–87, 191, 201
*Working Days: The Journal of "The Grapes
    of Wrath,"* 110, 112
World War I, 26–27
World War II, 124, 135, 149, 156
    John's works related to, 134–35,
        136–37, 138–41

Zanuck, Darryl, 163
Zapata, Emiliano, 149, 162

ABOUT THE AUTHOR

MILTON MELTZER has written more than one hundred books for young people and adults. He is the recipient of two awards honoring his lifetime body of work: the American Library Association's Laura Ingalls Wilder Award and the Catholic Library Association's Regina Medal. Five of his books have been finalists for the National Book Award. Many have been chosen for the honor lists of the National Council of Teachers of English, the National Council for the Social Studies, and the *New York Times* Best Books of the Year list.

His biographies of American writers include Langston Hughes, Herman Melville, Walt Whitman, Edgar Allan Poe, Mark Twain, Carl Sandburg, Emily Dickinson, Nathaniel Hawthorne, and Henry David Thoreau.

Meltzer and his wife, Hildy, live in New York. He is a member of the Authors Guild, American PEN, and the Organization of American Historians.